Prescription for Marriage

Contents

Introduction

Don't let this book threaten you.

You may feel anxious about exploring your marriage, but the avoidance of marriage maintenance can be more risky than doing it.

The real enemy of marriage is not conflict, incompatibility, or dissatisfaction but the unwillingness to acknowledge and solve problems.

Marital problems are inevitable but rarely terminal to a relationship when faced openly and honestly by partners who want to make their marriage work.

Marriage is not easy

Growing up and taking charge of your life is only a step toward genuine maturity. Learning to become a separate individual with your own identity is the developmental task of the "terrible two's" and the lively struggles of adolescence— and of mid-life adults for whom this task was not completed. But the achievement of autonomy is only a springboard to the more challenging and difficult task of adults—that of building and sustaining healthy relationships.

The ultimate goal of growing up is not a declaration of independence but the achievement of mutually satisfying relationships. Your life is likely to be as fulfilling as your relationships, no more, no less.

Human relationships are not easy. Competent individuals able to achieve success, power, wealth, position, or fame often struggle ineptly to build satisfying personal relationships.

Building a marriage relationship can be the most difficult and challenging task of adult life. Impersonal relationships are easier, less threatening, or demanding. The more intimate a relationship, the more maturity, commitment, and effort is required. G. B. Shaw once said it: "No relationship is better suited to produce conflict than marriage."

Marriage is worth the effort

The quality of your marriage relationship can be more important to the quality of your life than any other success or failure. You can rise above life's defeats and disappointments when you have someone who intimately and supportively shares your struggles. Conversely, extraordinary successes in life can become hollow if no one cares or shares them.

Although a successful marriage is not easy, its achievement has many rewards. A satisfying marriage relationship can be more important to health and well-being than nutrition, exercise, or body care. The importance of a satisfying marriage for physical well-being may be underemphasized among health professionals partly because relational data is difficult to measure, partly because the medical and scientific mind is not generally prone to give attention to personal relationships (ask their spouses), and partly because even competent professionals in the health sciences can feel mystified or inadequate when it comes to building or enriching marriages.

No easy answers

This book is written for those who are willing to face the challenge of building and enriching their marriage. This is an invitation to move beyond independence and autonomy to full maturity by taking the risks of relational growth. Some readers will be ready and eager for the challenge. Some will feel uneasy, vulnerable, and defensive. Perhaps no challenge in life is more risky, more demanding, or more rewarding.

You may be disappointed with this book if you are hoping for easy answers that eliminate work and risk. Building a marriage is like learning to play piano or golf. You may experience some immediate satisfactions as you begin, but the best rewards come only with persistent long term effort.

A life-long successful marriage does not come automatically with the marriage license. A satisfying relationship requires growth and maturity. There is no other way. But there is help.

Practical help

This book provides resources for building or enriching the four essential components of every relationship:
1. Cooperation
2. Compatibility
3. Emotional support
4. Intimacy

These four relational "systems" need to function adequately for a complete and stable marriage. The major sections of this book address these components. Tuning up the four components can build a more satisfying relationship by preventing breakdowns, aligning expectations with reality, and removing obstacles.

"Love" and "commitment" are essential to healthy marriages and might be compared to the fuel that energizes the four components. Marriage is easiest when love is lively and strong. Commitment can sustain a marriage when love fails but only for a limited period of time. Real commitment is not merely the determination to stick together no matter what, but rather to face and overcome problems together.

Communication is the lubrication of marriage. A relationship tends to wear out, burn up, or freeze without the lubrication of adequate communication. A particular type of communication is needed for each of the four component parts. This book is designed to help you talk with your partner in ways that lubricate cooperation, compatibility, emotional support, and intimacy.

Symptoms, diagnosis, and prescription

This book identifies twenty-six issues faced by most couples at some point in their relationship. Each issue begins with a description of its "symptoms," feelings, or experiences that signal a need for attention. A "diagnosis" follows which identifies underlying problems or issues to which the symptoms point. Each section concludes with a "prescription" for building or enriching your relationship so that the symptoms can be overcome and underlying issues resolved.

Symptoms

Every "symptom" listed at the beginning of a section may not fit every couple. If one or more "symptoms" do fit your relationship, you are likely to benefit from further exploration of the section. You may need to rephrase, however, a symptom description to fit your own experience because of the uniqueness of your relationship.

Take care not to defend against identifying symptoms as your own as if this were to admit a serious problem in your relationship. These symptoms are common to almost all marriages. A good marriage is not free from such experiences or feelings but rather faces them, talks about them, and finds solutions.

Diagnosis

An objective viewpoint can help when dealing with personal relationships. You need to know that your marital problems are not singular to you but universal among couples and have been addressed and resolved by others. You need to know that there are practical guidelines for understanding and responding to your situation.

The diagnostic information provided may not fit precisely your particular symptoms. But don't move on too quickly. You may need to expand or alter the diagnostic data to shed light on your situation. Each relationship is unique. Allow yourself to become a relational diagnostician for your own marriage by attempting to describe your issues in objective, universal terms.

Prescription

The practical suggestions provided for dealing with each issue are derived from my own clinical work and that of my students. They are actual experiences of spouses and couples. They work. Of course, some suggestions work better for some couples than do others.

Some prescriptive suggestions may meet with your resistance. Of course, thinking for yourself and trusting the wisdom of your own experiences is healthy and mature. If you have alternative solutions that work better for you, don't fight success. On the other hand, an overly rigid perspective can keep problems from being solved. Let yourself be stretched. Free yourself to try something new even if it seems difficult, strange, or inappropriate. Allow yourself to experiment with new approaches to old problems.

Suggested prescriptions or solutions will be disappointing if you expect too much from your marital relationship or if your goals are unrealistic. Marriage cannot solve all of your problems, satisfy all of your needs, fulfill all of your dreams, or make your life worth living. Some spouses spend a lifetime in a frustrating, self-defeating effort to shape their partner and their marriage to measure up to an unrealistic ideal. This book will not enable you to achieve the impossible, but it will help you make the most of what you have. And that is all that can be done with any marriage.

How to use this book

Although spouses can certainly benefit by applying this book to their relationship on an individual basis, couples are likely to achieve best results by a shared exploration of issues and answers. Keep this book in a handy place on your coffee table, by your bed, or perhaps in your bathroom, wherever you and your mate are most likely to pick it up. The treatment of each issue is kept relatively short so that it can be read in a few minutes. Fold the page or put a mark at an issue that you want your spouse to read. Invite your partner to do the same. Set some times aside for the two of you to talk about it.

Your spouse may be reluctant to read or discuss this book with you. Some partners find dealing with personal relationships to be uncomfortable or even painful and escape by avoiding such discussions. Don't force it. But don't withdraw, either. Use patience, not pressure. Keep the invitation open. Look for opportunities to talk about your relationship when you are both relaxed and feeling positive about each other so that discomfort and defensiveness are less likely to be a problem.

Chapter 1

You Want to Work on your Relationship

Symptoms

You know when your marriage is working and when you are dissatisfied, but you do not know exactly how to strengthen or build it. One or more of the following statements apply.

You or your partner . . .

. . . might be willing to "work" on your relationship if you knew what would help.

. . . may have tried to work on your relationship to make it better but your best efforts proved unproductive.

. . . may be puzzled or mystified by relationships and therefore have difficulty understanding what makes a marriage work.

. . . may come to rely on impulse, hunches, or blind luck in your marriage because you don't know how to assess or build a relationship.

. . . may be ready to explore the essential components of a relationship in order to affirm, enrich, or build your marriage.

Diagnosis

Many people find close personal relationships to be mystifying, complicated, and risky. A satisfying marriage seems to depend on physical attraction and emotional responses not subject to reason. Even if spouses are willing to explore and alter some of their own ways of relating, they cannot predict the reaction of a mate.

Not surprisingly, many spouses retreat from exploring their relationship. Some feel inadequate. Others have been hurt by a spouse and feel vulnerable. Still others fear exposing personal flaws. The lack of a practical basic understanding of how relationships work can foster such reluctance.

When a marriage is not working satisfactorily, spouses sometimes make random efforts to improve it without really knowing how a relationship works. Efforts to enrich their relationships can feel as futile and frustrating as a non-mechanic dealing with a stalled automobile. He opens the hood, pulls and pushes on wires, adjusts screws, and taps randomly on the unresponsive engine. The result is probably more harmful than helpful.

Looking at the mass of engine parts can be threatening or overwhelming to a person mystified by motors. If the essential systems were understood—ignition, fuel, cooling, lubrication, etc.—the engine would be demystified and a practical assessment of the problem might be possible. Similarly, human relationships have component parts that need to be kept in working condition. When relational systems are understood, relationships become less mystifying and more manageable. When spouses understand how their relationship works, they also understand what is needed when it is not working satisfactorily.

Prescription

Learn the following four relational systems essential to every satisfying marriage: 1. Cooperation, 2. Compatibility,

3. Emotional support, and 4. Intimacy. Love and commitment are also important, especially for getting through tough times, but they cannot sustain a relationship in the long run if the four relational systems break down.

Use these systems to help clarify how your relationship is working and what you can do to affirm, strengthen, or rebuild it. Begin to explore your own relationship as you read.

Each section and issue of this book is designed to help you solve problems or enrich your relationship with respect to one of these systems.

1. *Cooperation.* Explore how each of you deals with conflict or disagreement. Do conversations become argumentative? Do disagreements become hassles? Is decision-making unnecessarily difficult? Does disappointment, frustration, or anger build a wall between you? Marriage is not a competitive sport. Couples need to converse so that neither feels put down or defensive. Couples need to make decisions so that both partners are understood, respected, and satisfied with the results. Couples need to deal with conflict so that both win. Spouses need to define relational problems in terms of their own behavior and avoid attempts to change a partner. Cooperation eliminates the use of blaming, pressuring, demanding, hassling, or nagging to resolve conflict. Teamwork is basic.

2. *Compatibility.* Explore your success in building a shared lifestyle that feels like home to both partners while accepting differences in values, personalities, and family backgrounds. No couple is ever really compatible. Important differences are inevitable if only because one partner is male and the other female. Other differences result from family background and personality types. Of course some couples have more similarities than others. If you married someone with similar values and a cultural, educational, religious, social, and economic background much like your own, adjustments may be less demanding. If you married some-

one more different, you may experience more excitement and growth but you will probably have to work harder at building a shared lifestyle. In either case, building compatibility means accepting and affirming your similarities and differences and creatively combining them into a shared lifestyle that genuinely feels like home to you both.

3. *Emotional support.* Explore your patterns of giving and receiving the personal support you want and need from each other. Couples need to love each other into becoming their best selves. Everyone needs people who will listen, understand, affirm, hold, or provide support, especially when feeling down or hurting. About half of your emotional support can be expected from a spouse, half from other family and friends. When emotional support is not adequately provided in a marriage, it is sought elsewhere. Extramarital affairs often originate in the search for emotional support rather than for sex.

Couples can learn to understand the kind of emotional support each wants and needs from the other and to respond in genuinely helpful ways. Caring and good intentions are not enough. You may try to be helpful but saying or doing the wrong thing can make matters worse. You need to learn to listen, empathize, convey understanding, touch, or hold in ways that support and affirm without undermining your partner's feelings or competence.

4. *Intimacy.* Explore how you and your partner seek and avoid conversational, emotional, and physical intimacy. Most people marry yearning for a special kind of closeness—a sharing of inner worlds of thought and emotion. But while yearning for personal and emotional intimacy, you also fear it. Some spouses yearn more, some fear it more.

Intimacy requires an open, spontaneous, free-flowing expression of thoughts and feelings that makes each person unique. When intimacy breaks down, couples can share the same home and bed and still feel like strangers to each other. Intimacy requires a relational climate of acceptance, free from judgment or criticism, free from pressure or coercion, free from defensiveness or resistance. You can learn to build the level of intimacy you desire in your conversation, your expression of emotion, your physical touching, and sexual relating.

Burn these four systems into your memory: cooperation, compatibility, emotional support, and intimacy. Use them first and mostly to affirm the strengths in your relationship. When you are feeling positive about your relationship, identify the system you would most want to enrich. Set goals. Be specific. Sections of this book are designed to help with specific issues in each of these four systems.

Chapter 2

You Want to Avoid Marriage Maintenance

Symptoms

This book makes you or your partner uncomfortable; you would like to avoid dealing with your relationship. You are also aware that not dealing with your relationship has risks. One or more of the following apply.

One or both of you . . .

. . . would like to toss this book aside, yet you continue reading partly because you know that a satisfying marriage is important to your health and happiness.

. . . is undecided about your willingness to tolerate the risk and discomfort of exploring your relationship.

. . . would like to believe that a satisfying marriage is possible without direct effort, that a happy marriage comes as a gift or by luck.

. . . tends to think that if your marriage is not satisfying, you are simply a victim of misfortune. There is nothing you can do.

. . . avoids exploring or working on your marriage because you feel vulnerable, inadequate, or defensive when it comes to personal relationships.

. . . is still reading this book because you suspect that marriage maintenance may be a lot less uncomfortable than marital breakdown.

Diagnosis

A lifelong, trouble-free marriage does not come automatically with a marriage license. Yet many spouses would prefer almost anything to working on their marriage relationship. Some become uncomfortable whenever conversations become personal. Some become defensive, uncertain that they can measure up to the spouse's emotional needs. Some insist their marriage needs no attention. Some are at a loss to know how to explore a relationship.

At the same time, although reluctant to talk about it, they know that their marriage is important, perhaps more important than anything else in life. They know they need a partner to enjoy their successes when life is going well and to provide care and support when life gets rough. Life would be flat, lonely, and boring without their spouse.

They would like to think that their marriage can work without thought or effort. When their relationship does not work, they tend to think of themselves as a victim of misfortune. Such thinking allows them to avoid responsibility for making their relationship work.

Building a satisfying marriage is not easy. Success is not guaranteed. But few achievements in life are more important or fulfilling than a satisfying relationship.

Couples don't just fall into a good marriage. A stable, satisfying, and lasting relationship requires thoughtfulness and effort. Spouses who think they have an effortlessly successful relationship need to check it out. Perhaps their partners are doing all the work.

Even spouses who put a high value on their marriage often fail to do what is needed to sustain it. Couples can put more time, energy, and money caring for their car than for their marriage. A relationship needs servicing and maintenance just as much.

Premarital preparation or counseling can be helpful for establishing a healthy marriage. But efforts to build a relationship become more important after the wedding. The challenges and requirements of marriage rarely come clear until after the erotic stardust mellows into the demands of everyday life. "In service training" works as well in marriage as it does for other vocations.

Couples need to assume that attending to their relationship is essential even when this means discomfort, vulnerability, or risk. Working on a relationship may be most important when spouses are least inclined to do it.

Marriage maintenance is a lifelong task. No marriage ever "arrives." Marriages need to change and grow just as individuals do. Marriages churn and adjust through stages. Relationships need to survive and grow through highs and lows, excitement and depression, being in-love and out-of-love, and through all the critical transitions in between.

Prescription

Accept the challenges of marriage without illusions or unrealistic expectations. Marriage is not easy.

Relinquish the notion that finding the "right" partner assures a happy and harmonious marriage. Whomever you choose for a partner, you will have to work at your relationship.

Do not assume that a good relationship is trouble-free. A good marriage is simply one that deals with problems effectively.

Let the following statements, to which almost all marital specialists would agree, motivate you to do maintenance work on your marriage.

1. All marriages have "problems."
2. All couples are "incompatible" in the sense that part-

ners inevitably have significant differences.

3. All couples feel "out of love" sometimes.

4. All marriages have built-in conflict.

5. All partners sometimes wish they had married someone else.

6. All marriages experience difficult periods of transitions.

7. No marriage is consistently satisfying to both partners.

Take risks beyond your comfort zone to explore and enrich your relationship. Challenge yourself to build cooperation, compatibility, emotional support, and intimacy as a jogger pushes beyond previous limits to increase speed and distance. What is not comfortable at first can become comfortable and satisfying with persistence.

Perhaps your spouse will agree to set time aside regularly to talk about your relationship together. If you do, here are some suggestions:

1. Select a time when you both are well fed, well rested, and feeling good about your marriage. Postpone marriage maintenance when you are feeling cold, distant, hurt, or angry.

2. Begin by talking about what feels good about your marriage, what has been working well, and what you have appreciated recently about your spouse.

3. Marriage maintenance needs to be done without pressures, defensiveness, accusing, excusing, or blaming. If either of you is getting "uptight," work it through or postpone your discussion to another time.

This book is written as a "user's manual" for marriage and provides a description of a variety of marital issues that require attention. Relevant sections can help focus your efforts.

Be willing to try new behavior. Give marriage maintenance a priority in your life. Your marriage is worth the effort. What is more important in the long run?

Chapter 3

You Need Relational Skills

Symptoms

This chapter is for spouses who have difficulty talking to each other. After only a few moments of conversation, you or your partner begin to feel misunderstood, discounted, put down, defensive, or argumentative. One or more of the following statements apply.

One or both of you . . .

. . . has a mind that wanders while your partner talks.

. . . considers what you will say next instead of listening to your partner.

. . . attends to the words of your partner but ignores important underlying feelings.

. . . does not know if you are heard and understood when you talk because your partner does not respond.

. . . sometimes sulks or gets noisy in order to get a response.

. . . cannot disagree without becoming disagreeable.

. . . finds satisfaction in pointing out flaws or inconsistencies in what your partner says.

. . . intellectualizes without revealing what you really think, feel, or want.

Diagnosis

Love is not enough. Well intentioned, loving couples may have difficulty talking, sharing, discussing problems, making decisions, or simply having fun together because they cannot communicate effectively. Lacking skills, couples can be locked into self-defeating conversational patterns without awareness of what they are doing or how to change it.

At the heart of the problem is a difficulty with communication. Words can hide as well as reveal. Words can be fired as missiles or piled up as a protective wall. Words can be misinterpreted, ignored, or discounted. Words can be taken as captured booty to be used in a counterattack.

Most people grow up without any training in communication or relational skills. Couples need a license to get married, but are not required to pass a competency test to qualify.

Most of us relate to our spouse much like our parents related to each other. If our parents were good models, we have a head start. Although most spouses admire and respect their parents, many would like to build a better relationship than their parents had. But few opportunities to build new relational skills are sought or offered.

Basic communication skills are needed.

Prescription

Successful communication requires two sets of skills: receiving and sending.

Receiving skills include:

1. Attending—using your body posture and eye contact to show that you are giving your full attention.

2. Listening—keeping focused on what your partner is saying without letting your mind wander or considering what you will say in return.

3. Respect and acceptance—taking into full account the

wisdom of your partner's experience while receiving the thoughts, feelings, and desires of your partner without judgment.

4. Communicating understanding—reflecting back to your partner what you hear and understand both to show that you are listening and to correct misunderstanding.

Sending skills include:

1. Appropriate assertiveness—expressing your own thoughts, feelings, and desires without apologies or defensiveness while at the same time avoiding aggressiveness.

2. Self-revealing—expressing what is really going on inside you even when feeling vulnerable or embarrassed so that your partner can know and understand you.

3. Straight talk—being clear and straightforward, not hiding behind a wall of words, lecturing, teasing, intellectualizing, withdrawing, or sulking to avoid dealing with a sensitive subject.

4. Immediacy—talking about what is going on between the two of you when it is happening especially when communication is not working well.

Such basic communication skills may be difficult for one of you and effortless for the other. Much depends on the parental or other role models you imitated while growing up. However easy or difficult, you can learn to use communication skills.

Ask your partner which skills would be most helpful to your relationship. Then identify one or more skills you want to develop or improve. Determine to sharpen those skills in your conversations practicing them with others in your social network as well as in your marriage.

The rewards can be enormous.

Chapter 4

When Teamwork Breaks Down

Symptoms

You or your partner feel that you are not on the same team, that you are pulling in different directions. At least one of the following statements applies.

One or both of you . . .

. . . feels a vague tension in your stomach after only a few minutes of conversation. You feel put down, discounted, or challenged.

. . . tends to press harder to make a point, repeat yourself, speak louder, or more forcefully when your partner does not agree.

. . . feels inwardly defeated when your partner disagrees; you need to be reassured, to be vindicated, to win, to be right, or at least not to be wrong.

. . . often contends for what is equitable, right, or fair.

. . . is unsatisfied with the way conflict is resolved; the satisfaction in winning does not last and you don't like to lose.

. . . finds making decisions together difficult; you win or lose rather than find a mutually satisfying consensus.

... feels that your judgment and opinions are not adequately respected in the decision-making process.

... is frustrated that so much energy is expended in pulling against each other rather than used for mutual achievement or enjoyment.

Diagnosis

A research project reported by a health insurance newsletter indicated that the average couple cannot converse for more than seven minutes without one or both feeling put down, defensive, or argumentative. The most casual conversation on a non-controversial subject can become an argument, undermining cooperation, harmony, warmth, or mutual support.

Competition can erupt as simply as this:

> "Remember last Wednesday when we. . . . "
> "No dear, that was Thursday."
> "No, I distinctly remember it was Wednesday because. . . . "
> "Well, you may remember it that way, but. . . . "

Whether it was Wednesday or Thursday does not matter; winning the argument, or, at least not losing, gets to be important.

Sometimes the competition is hidden underneath the conversation:

> "You don't know what it's like out there fighting the battle of the beltway every day." (I've got it worse than you do, and I need appreciation and emotional support.)
> "It can't be as bad as fighting construction at the shopping mall with the incessant emotional demands of two small children." (It's as bad or worse for me; I'm the one that needs appreciation and emotional support.)

Both partners yearn to be heard and understood and to

feel the support and appreciation of the other. Both are likely to be frustrated and resentful when their claim meets a competitive counterclaim. Both feel unloved and unappreciated. Both want the other to yield. Neither may recognize competition as the problem.

Frustration and dissatisfaction are inevitable when competition becomes a primary way of relating. Neither partner can win. If one spouse presses hard and achieves a reluctant compliance, the victory will bring no lasting satisfaction. The "winner" always pays a price. A defeated, perhaps resentful, spouse will extract payment sooner or later, one way or another. A spouse that always needs to "win" is married to a "loser" and becomes one in the process.

Frustrated and separated by a wall of competition, some couples seek professional help. Unfortunately, the counseling process is often defeated as spouses compete to enlist the counselor as an ally against the mate. Competition continues as they compete in their therapy over defining their problem, determining fault, and pressuring each other to change. Both can become hypersensitive about whose "side" the counselor takes. Of course, the counselor needs to end the competition, not enter it.

Some spouses grow up in competitive families and enjoy the emotional and intellectual interaction of a lively argument. A competitive hassle is fine as long as both partners enjoy it. Some people engage in arguments just as others enjoy tennis or chess. But competition, whether verbal or athletic, is for recreation, not for solving problems.

Sometimes spouses blame their partners for creating hassles. Such blaming is only another competitive ploy. Hassling is not possible unless both participate. Although some spouses are skillful at "hooking" their mates into an argument, nobody can force competition on an aware and unwilling partner. Spouses avoid competition by changing themselves, not by changing the mate.

Arguing cannot successfully solve problems because competition tends to have winners and loser. Winning at the expense of your partner does not bring lasting satisfaction. And losing brings frustration and resentment. Couples need to solve problems so that both win. In fact, unless both win, nobody wins.

Prescription

Marriage is not a competitive sport. Married partners are on the same team. You need to pull together and for one another rather than push against each other.

Be aware early on of hassles as they develop. Identify the muscular tightness, voice tones, or inner pressure that signal the pushing and pulling of competition with your partner. Such awareness allows you to decide if you want the satisfactions that come with an argument or would rather converse without competition. Of course, if you both want the emotional engagement and intellectual challenge of an argument, as some couples do, feel free to enjoy whatever satisfactions you get from it.

However, if you want to solve a problem or if you don't want to hassle, you need to look for alternatives. Nobody can make you argue if you are genuinely unwilling. However, learning the attitudes and responses that avoid competitive arguments may require time and practice if this is new to you.

You can learn to talk to each other, even when you disagree, without tension, argument, or defensiveness. You can grant to each other the right to have your own thoughts and feelings. You can hear and understand your partner whether or not you agree. Here are some guidelines for noncompetitive conversation from an excellent therapist and mentor, H. D. Johns:

1. Listen attentively and carefully.

2. You do not need to agree. Accept different viewpoints as inevitable and healthy.

3. Do not criticize, defend yourself, or apologize— whatever your spouse may say or not say.

4. Show that you understand and respect what your partner says whether or not you agree. A typical response: "I understand; it is important for me to know that you feel that way."

If you follow these guidelines carefully, you will be able to talk for long periods of time without hassling. If competition seems to recur in spite of your best efforts, perhaps you need to look for some underlying satisfaction you might derive from it that may lie outside of your awareness.

Chapter 5
Conflict Becomes Divisive

Symptoms
This chapter is for spouses that have difficulty working through disagreements to their mutual satisfaction. One or more of the following statements apply.

One or both of you . . .

. . . is unaware of or denies conflict in your relationship.

. . . hides thoughts, feelings, or desires that might cause conflict.

. . . yields, reluctantly, before conflict is expressed.

. . . says "yes" when you mean "no" so that resentment builds up inwardly.

. . . seems to have an inner need to prevail and control in conflict.

. . . uses self-defeating "weapons" in conflict such as nagging, threatening, screaming, sulking, hitting, withholding affection, or the silent treatment.

. . . kindles an argument for its own sake—though probably outside of awareness; you would rather hassle than suffer boredom.

. . . prefers the emotional engagement that comes with

open conflict to feelings of loneliness.

. . . futilely tries to achieve closeness through conflict.

Diagnosis

Conflict is inevitable in every relationship. A cooperative couple does not have less conflict than a hassling one. The difference results from how a couple deals with disagreement.

Most couples are uncomfortable with conflict. Many will avoid it at almost any cost. They think of conflict as unloving, destructive, even, perhaps, an indication of serious marital difficulty. Unfortunately, the effort to avoid conflict can result in denial, manipulation, excessive controlling, and over-adapting.

Denying conflict does not eliminate it. Real harmony does not result from burying differences. Hiding conflicting thoughts, feelings, and attitudes only preserves an illusion of oneness. In exchange for an external peace, partners forfeit authenticity and closeness and build up resentment.

Some couples avoid the expression of conflict by playing complementary roles: one controls, the other yields. Which partner actually prevails is not as obvious as it might seem. The controlling partner rarely achieves genuine cooperation and even less affection. The hidden resentment of the yielding partner is likely to have the last word in subtle ways. Sometimes it builds quietly toward an explosion. In any case, such couples maintain an illusion of unity by avoiding open confrontation. Unfortunately, though harmonious on the surface, they may not be able to enjoy authentic cooperative teamwork.

Some couples enjoy the emotional interaction of a lively argument. Emotional confrontation sometimes temporarily renews intimacy and overcomes barriers to cooperation. But fighting is not a method for solving problems or resolving genuine differences. Arguing tends to result in a "winner" and a "loser" which, in personal relationships, usually means two losers. You cannot genuinely win at the expense of your partner.

Couples need to deal with conflict so that the individual thinking and feeling of both partners is understood and respected. Both need to participate in creative problem-solving. In the end, both must win or both will lose.

Creative problem-solving can achieve much more than equitable but unsatisfying compromises. When marriage is seen as a fifty-fifty give-and-take, one or both partners will soon feel cheated. Couples can usually expect to resolve conflict so that both achieve about 80 percent of what is wanted.

Many spouses possess problem-solving skills gained through education or job training and only need to apply them to marital conflict. When conflict occurs, a couple can ask each other: do we fight or do we problem-solve? Remember that fighting is for recreation if you enjoy it; problem-solving is for resolving conflict.

Prescription

Don't compete. If you want to deal with conflict effectively, you need to solve problems in a climate free of competition. Nobody wins. Nobody loses.

Do not compete over defining a problem. Resist defining a disagreement so that your partner is at fault. Blaming does not solve problems. You are each entitled to your definition of the problem. You do not need to agree; you only need to understand each other. For example, take turns describing a problem as the other sees it.

Do not debate about what is "fair." Solutions to conflict do not need to be fair. They only need to work. It might be "fair" if neither of you gets what you want, but it will not be satisfying. If you are creative, you can both get more than what is "fair."

When dealing with conflict, keep this question in focus: Accepting and respecting what each of us thinks, feels, and desires, how can we best satisfy what we each want and need?

You can solve problems effectively only in an emotional climate of mutual acceptance, respect, and cooperation. Discuss your conflicts and differences when you are both well fed, rested, and feeling good about each other and your relationship. Many partners possess problem-solving skills and only need the right emotional climate to employ them. The basic steps include:

1. Establish clearly what each needs or wants.

2. Suggest together as many alternatives as possible in which each gets as much of what is wanted as possible.

3. Select one of these alternative solutions that is acceptable to both.

4. Celebrate a mutual win.

5. Evaluate the results. Repeat the process if either becomes dissatisfied.

Creative problem-solving sometimes results in solutions that are more satisfying than what either spouse initially wanted.

Chapter 6

The Blaming Game

Symptoms

This chapter is for spouses who, inwardly or outwardly, tend to respond to frustration or disappointment by blaming their partner. One or more of the following statements will apply.

One or both of you . . .

. . . tends to determine who is at fault as a first reaction when something goes wrong.

. . . tends to become argumentative or defensive when dealing with a problem.

. . . would rather establish innocence than solve a problem.

. . . feels frustrated and defeated by attempts to motivate your partner to change a way of thinking or acting that causes a problem.

. . . feels victimized by your mate.

. . . is confident when problems arise that you could convince any jury that your partner is at fault.

. . . is convinced that your partner can change lifelong patterns of behavior to solve a problem—although you are not optimistic about being able to make such changes within yourself.

. . . tries to enlist others such as family, friends, or a marriage counselor as allies in convincing your partner to accept fault and make adjustments.

Diagnosis

Whether given or received, blaming does not solve problems or get spouses what they really want. Walls of separation tend to grow bigger as blaming escalates.

Yet many spouses respond to disappointment, dissatisfaction, or unhappiness in marriage by blaming the partner. Whenever anything goes wrong, the first response is to determine fault. Competition over determining fault is called the Blaming Game. The ups and downs, disappointments, and frustrations of marriage provides a fertile field for this contest in which nobody wins and everyone loses.

Indications that a couple is caught in the "Blaming Game" include:

1. Problems are not resolved even though solutions seem obvious.

2. Resistance and defensiveness surface even when partners intend to compromise or yield.

3. Spouses feel frustrated by an inability to motivate their partners to alter a way of thinking or behaving that seems obviously to be the problem.

4. One or both partners feel innocently oppressed or victimized by the other's behavior.

5. One or both partners are confident that any judge or jury in the country would agree with their assessment of the problem.

6. One or both believes that determining fault is an important step to solving a problem.

Some spouses blame directly and explicitly: "If you would only" . . . "why didn't you" . . . "why can't you" . . . "it's your fault" . . . etc. But most blame inwardly saying the same sort of things inside the head. Blaming, expressed or hidden, tends to build walls of judgment. Those blamed tend to dig trenches of defensiveness. Neither partner ever wins the blaming game. Everybody loses.

Some spouses enlist a marriage counselor as an ally in the blaming game. Many, perhaps most, couples entering marital therapy assume that the function of a counselor is to determine which spouse is at fault. The counselor is cast in the role of judge or jury. This rarely or never helps. A spouse found "guilty" is likely to appeal to a higher court, i.e., to family, friends or a more expensive therapist. The vindication of the "innocent" spouse brings no satisfying results. The real task of the counselor, of course, should not be to referee but to enable a couple to stop the game.

Patterns of blaming and defending often develop in childhood interaction with parents or siblings and are reinforced by non-constructive but familiar satisfactions. Blaming a partner helps maintain a self-image of innocence, shifts responsibility for problems, requires no personal change, and defends against feelings of inferiority. Such satisfactions may feel good for the moment and defend against self-criticism, guilt, or fear of failure.

Such gratification is short-lived. Blaming tends to build walls, create distance, and sustain a repetitious circle of counter-blaming and defensiveness.

Worst of all, blaming tends to result in an impasse in relational problems. If you define your marital dissatisfaction in terms of your partner's behavior, you keep your problems unsolvable since you cannot change your partner. If you try to resolve issues by changing your partner, you are stuck. Relational problems remain unsolvable until you stop blaming.

Prescription

If you want to break out of the blaming game, you need to redefine marital issues in terms of your own behavior.

You may resist this prescription. Such a solution may seem like "giving in." Perhaps you feel that you have already yielded too often. Now it is your partner's turn to do some giving.

You do not need to "give in" when redefining the problem in terms of your own behavior. For example, if you feel lonely, do not blame your partner for not talking to you and attempt to force more conversation. Tell your partner how you feel and what you want and invite a response, but do so without hassling. Then satisfy social needs with others that your partner is not able or willing to meet. This releases you from the frustrating and self-defeating task of trying to change your partner. You can learn to take care of yourself in ways that do not necessarily mean yielding to your partner.

Some resist redefining the problem in terms of their own behavior because that seems to put them at fault—which is back to the blaming game. Redefining in terms of your own behavior does not mean blaming yourself. If you are about to be hit by a truck running a stop sign, it will not help to blame the driver for your situation. You need to define the problem in terms of your own behavior and jump out of the way.

When you solve relational problems by altering your own behavior, you may be surprised and rewarded by your partner's response. Of course you cannot control your mate's reactions, but you may be surprised by your spouse's adjustments to what you do. When the blaming is gone and an accepting emotional climate prevails, growth and changes occur freely that rarely develop when couples are entrenched in the blaming game.

Chapter 7

Anger Builds Walls

Symptoms

Expressed or unexpressed, anger can get in the way of your closeness, harmony, and mutual caring. Anger may be an issue in your marriage if any of the following describe your relationship.

One or both of you . . .

. . . enjoys the emotional engagement that comes with expressing anger, but you do not experience the kind of closeness you want afterward.

. . . swallows, bottles, and avoids expressing anger, maintaining a surface harmony even when seething inside.

. . . suppresses it so well, you are no longer aware of your anger.

. . . maintains a "pressure cooker tranquility" in which anger is contained while it builds toward an explosion.

. . . sometimes seems to lose control of your anger.

. . . concludes that anger is an enemy of a loving relationship and so you suppress it in yourself and fear it in your partner.

. . . is aware at times of a wall of anger that gets in the

way of teamwork, caring, warmth, and closeness.

Diagnosis

Some spouses express anger openly and some never utter a harsh word. Either way, anger impacts on every relationship with or without awareness.

Anger helps some couples to get closer at least for a little while if it is expressed freely and openly. Venting anger can temporarily remove barriers to intimacy but it rarely produces long-term benefits.

Some spouses use anger to gain control, to compel their partners to listen, respond, and, perhaps, to yield in some way. But ultimately the kind of power that comes with anger is an illusion. Anger pushes the partner away and fails to achieve closeness, understanding, support, or cooperation. After an angry outburst has subsided, most spouses feel more frustrated, isolated, and powerless.

Other spouses avoid expressing anger as much as possible. They fear anger's destructive power. Some turn anger inward so that it festers inside the mind and stomach. Some bottle, collect, and store it for a later major guilt-free self-indulgence. Anger gets expressed one way or another, directly or indirectly.

Some relationships swing between a constrained calm and periodic rages. Controlled anger builds up like steam in a pressure cooker with an inoperative release valve. The relationship seems tranquil over a period of time, but inwardly anger builds up to an inevitable explosion. Outbursts resulting from anger buildup tend to be disproportionate to the precipitating event and misdirected toward an undeserving but vulnerable target.

Anger is inevitable in every relationship. Spouses have to do something with their anger each time they allow their partner to win an argument at their expense, each time they yield to avoid conflict, each time they feel rejected, put down, discounted, or in some way rendered impotent. They may maintain a pleasing and compliant exterior, but in the long run their anger will find a way to express itself, directly or indirectly, helpful or harmful, inside or outside of their awareness.

Married partners are likely to deal with anger much as their parents did. They express it, swallow it, store it, collect it, or restrain and explode much as their parents did when they were growing up. Some imitate parents; some react by attempting to do the opposite.

Partners that "swallow" anger tend to punish their spouses and themselves indirectly. Although "nice and pleasant" on the surface, they may gain excessive weight, become uncooperative, wallow in low self-esteem, erect subtle barriers to affection, avoid intimacy or play "games" with sex. Since anger is denied, all this can be done with little or no awareness.

Partners that suppress anger and explode like a pressure cooker without a release valve defeat the relationship both ways. Closeness and warmth are not likely while anger is building up pressure inside. The inevitable explosion consumes enormous energy without solving problems. Anger needs to be expressed appropriately, directly, and strategically to resolve issues as they occur.

Anger is expressed violently and destructively by spouses who experience anger as rage. Such outbursts are often a defense against feeling used, discounted, or powerlessness and can be defined as "impotency rages." A raging person is able to feel powerful, frightening, and controlling but only for a little while. The power dissipates with the rage and remorse augments the return of powerlessness. Damage must be compensated. The power experienced in rage is an illusion. Such "impotency rages" sometimes result in child or spousal abuse.

Some partners refrain from expressing anger directly but

tend to remember each grievance in detail. They carefully build up and store a "resentment collection" which can be sorted and reviewed periodically. All is calm on the surface until a resentment collection is "cashed in" for guilt-free satisfactions—a spending spree, an affair, a separation, whatever. A resentment collection is almost always destructive, and can be very difficult for some spouses to surrender.

Some spouses use anger or the threat of anger as a weapon. Often outside of awareness, anger is employed to control a partner, coerce change, get compliance, or to punish. But such attempts are self-defeating. With rare exceptions, any attempt to get something with anger pays too high a price and results in long-term loss—loss of intimacy, warmth, communication, or emotional support.

Although anger can be a problem that builds a wall, it can also be an opportunity, providing awareness of what needs attention, stirring to action, and motivating to deal with problems as they occur. Couples need to make their anger work for them and not against them.

Anger, like volatile fuel in a tank, is useless or destructive when bottled up or exploded in mass. Like fuel, anger needs a steady outlet in manageable and productive amounts to be useful energy; it needs to provide thrust at the right time in the right place and direction.

Prescription

Stop using anger to control your partner. Whatever you try to force from your partner with anger is not worth having, at least not at that price. If you want harmony, cooperation, support, warmth, closeness, or romance, you will not get it with coercive anger.

Determine to use anger to build and enrich your relationship. Although this may not be easy, your efforts will be richly rewarded. Winners in life and love learn to use anger-energy to achieve their goals.

You will probably find some of the following steps more challenging than others. If you have difficulty dealing with anger, identify the steps that give you the most trouble and concentrate your effort there.

1. Allow yourself to feel your anger. Do not block it, disguise it, or replace it with other feelings, i.e., hurt, sad, or scared. You are entitled to your feelings. Feeling anger will not damage your partner, your relationship, or yourself.

2. Allow yourself to know what you want. What you get with eruptions of raw anger is probably not what you really want. Determine what you want instead, i.e., more closeness, sharing, cooperation, attention, affirmation, warmth, support, understanding, security, romance, or fun.

3. Determine a course of action that will get you what you really want. Do not demand instant success, but be determined to win in the long run. Do not waste your anger bottling it up or dissipating it in an explosion. Use it as productive energy to motivate, take risks, try new behaviors, and to do what it takes to achieve your goal.

4. Don't waste your anger energy. How you use your anger energy largely determines whether you are a winner or loser in marriage and in life. Don't misdirect it, for example, at the dog instead of your spouse or at your mate instead of your boss.

Don't hold the illusion that you can "lose your temper" in the sense that your anger goes out of your control. Although it may feel that way, there is a fraction of a second when you decide whether or not to let go. Take charge of that decision. Instead of exploding, determine to use your anger realistically to achieve what you really want.

Anger is a useful gift and an opportunity when used in this way. Remember, however, that you can never win at the expense of your partner. Take care that getting what you want always means a win for your partner as well as for yourself. Your life together needs to work for both of you.

Chapter 8

Your Partner Fails
to Measure Up

Symptoms

This chapter is for spouses who are disappointed in their mates and in their marriages or have a spouse that feels that way. If so, one or more of the following statements would apply.

You or your partner . . .

. . . yearn for a mate and marriage that fits your ideal more closely, that measures up to your hopes and dreams.

. . . is frustrated with your mate's failure to share your interests as you think an ideal mate should.

. . . regrets your choice of a mate though you may not admit it even to yourself.

. . . is frustrated and disappointed in your attempts to make changes in your mate to fit your ideal more closely.

. . . sometimes considers the ultimate solution: separate from your spouse and find someone who measures up to your ideal.

Diagnosis

The perfect mate cannot be found. Every spouse is

married to someone that seriously disappoints them in important ways. Changing spouses or trying to alter the one you have will not result in the ideal relationship.

As long as spouses struggle, agonize, argue, or fight in an effort to have their partners measure up to their ideal, they won't be able to enjoy what is good and working in their relationship.

Many spouses carry images of an ideal mate from youth and cherish mental pictures of sharing what is important to them with their special person. When romantic illusions yield to reality, however, couples discover that their partners have neither the aptitude nor inclination to measure up to these ideals. They become aware that their mate and their marriage will never fulfill their ideal. They feel disappointed and cheated. Their commitment may be shaken.

If spouses make an effort to recreate their partners into their ideal mate, their frustration is likely to increase. A partner might oblige on the surface, but basic personality characteristics, aptitudes, and preferences remain. Spouses who are determined to get their partners to measure up to their ideal are likely to spend a lifetime hassling, blaming, nagging, demanding, threatening, and pressuring with whatever leverage they can find. Others may simply suffer and endure in silence. Either way, the result is chronic dissatisfaction and frustration.

Some decide to end their marriage when expectations fall short of fulfillment. They search for a different mate who will measure up to their ideal. Unfortunately, that ideal spouse does not exist and therefore cannot be found. The search sometimes leads through a series of partners resulting only in further disappointment and, perhaps, growing loneliness and cynicism. The effort is self-defeating.

There is no perfect mate. No marriage measures up to the ideal in every way. The romantic ideal must yield to maturity. No one marries a mirror image of oneself. Every marriage partner will have unique interests, ideals, aptitudes, inclinations, stress tolerance, personality characteristics, values, and life-style preferences different from one's own. Partners need to accept these differences and surrender every effort to recreate the spouse in one's own image.

Some mates and marriages come relatively close to the ideal. Even then, some spouses suffer so much over their minor disappointments that they are unable to enjoy what is good. Spouses need to accept what falls short of the ideal so that they can make the most of what works in their marriage.

Of course, no one needs to be a victim of their partner's inability to measure up to the ideal in every way. Couples can enjoy together what works well in their relationships. They can enjoy separately and individually what they do not and cannot share. What cannot be enjoyed with a spouse can be shared with someone else.

Prescription

You may need to do some grieving over the failure of your spouse to measure up to your hopes and ideals. All spouses do at some point in their marriage.

Stages in the grieving process have come to be familiar: denial, bargaining, depression, anger, and, finally, acceptance. You may experience some or all of these as you learn to accept the limits and disappointments of your marriage.

Grieving brings healing. Grieving is a natural and healthy process that allows you to move beyond disappointment or loss to a new beginning. No matter who you married, you will have to grieve and move beyond the disappointment over the failure of your spouse to measure up to your ideal. Only by letting go of your frustrations and disappointment over what does not work will you be free to celebrate and enjoy what does.

Instead of learning to live creatively with your disappointments, you may be tempted to try to change your partner to measure up to your ideal. Resist this temptation no matter how enticing it may seem. Attempting to change your partner will keep you focused on your disappointment, add to your frustration, and prevent growth or movement in your relationship. It requires maturity and courage to face the reality that no marriage, no spouse, no life will measure up to your ideal expectations.

Letting go of your disappointments and accepting reality can free you to enjoy the possibilities your marriage offers, to allow yourself to focus on what you can enjoy in your partner, and to make the most of what you have in common. You can see the proverbial glass as half full rather than half empty. You can enjoy what works rather than suffer about what doesn't.

Do not become a victim of your mate or the shortcomings in your marriage. Your life is not limited by what you can share with your partner. You can enjoy with someone else what you cannot enjoy with your spouse. A sports loving mate with a non-athletic spouse can find others for golf or tennis. A fine arts loving spouse with an unappreciative mate can find others to tour shows or museums. A gregarious spouse with a withdrawing mate can build a social network of friends.

Free yourself to make the most of what you have by grieving away your disappointment over what you don't have.

Chapter 9

You Seem Incompatible

Symptoms

You or your partner sometimes wonder if you are right for each other. One or more of the following descriptions fits at least in a general way.

One or both of you . . .

. . . feels frustrated by your different habits or lifestyle preferences: for example, one saves while the other spends; one is prompt while the other is tardy; one is formal while the other is casual; one is decisive while the other procrastinates; one likes the arts; the other sports; one likes classical, the other country.

. . . senses that underlying values pull you in different directions: for example, one lives to get while the other to give; one is religious while the other is secular; one wants freedom, the other commitment.

. . . is frustrated by contrasting personality traits: for example, one thinks while the other feels; one lives in the present while the other anticipates the future; one is social while the other is private; one likes to make decisions in advance while the other prefers to keep options open.

. . . becomes aware that the life you are developing does not feel like "home."

. . . comes to feel that marital adjustments demand too much.

. . . begins to conclude that you cannot be true to yourself and be married to your partner.

Diagnosis

Spouses are never fully compatible.

Males and females are different from each other not only physically, but also mentally, emotionally, and relationally.

Spouses are also likely to have differences in values, lifestyle preferences, and personality.

Spouses have different childhood experiences and make different early life decisions in the context of different family backgrounds. Thus they inevitably have differences in basic fundamental values and priorities that determine how each deals with marriage, money, religion, parenting, time use, etc.

Spouses develop lifestyle preferences and habits that become deeply ingrained and do not change with marriage. Differences with respect to home decor, pets, kitchen and bathroom care, personal habits, clothing styles, taste in music or TV, choice of friends, and all the other "little things" that disappoint or irritate can prevent one or both spouses from feeling authentically and comfortably "at home."

Spouses can also be different in personality characteristics even if they have similar family backgrounds, values, and lifestyle preferences. For example, one may be emotional, the other analytical; one enjoys the present, the other fantasizes the future; one is energized when socializing, the other exhausted; one wants a predictable life, the other likes surprises.

Although some have more similarities than others, no

couple is ever naturally compatible in the sense that partners share all values, priorities, lifestyle preferences, habits,
and personality characteristics. Even if it were to exist, such
compatibility would be flat, boring, lacking in challenge,
variety, and romance.

Compatibility is not something some couples have while
others do not. It is something couples achieve or fail to
achieve. Compatibility is something couples build out of
their differences.

Couples with wider differences tend to experience more
excitement and romance in their relationship, but may need
to put more effort into compatibility issues than those that
have more in common.

Couples with more similarity may find compatibility more
readily achieved, but need to keep their life and relationship
stimulating and challenging with outside activities.

Compatibility requires the achievement of a life together
that feels genuinely like home to both partners. An effortless
compatibility is an illusion. Authentic compatibility is not
achieved when one partner simply yields to preserve
harmony or avoid conflict. Unless both partners feel genuinely "at home" in the marriage, dissatisfaction is likely to
mount.

Couples need to learn to benefit both from similarities
and differences and to build a satisfying compatibility that
offers both security, familiarity, and growth.

Prescription

Here are some suggestions for building compatibility.

1. Do not attempt to build compatibility by remaking your
partner into someone more like yourself.

2. Accept and affirm your differences. Your differences
probably added mystery, romance, and excitement that first
attracted you to your partner. Rekindle your appreciation for

the "differentness" of your partner by recalling your initial fascination.

3. Let your differences keep you growing. Determine to be stretched rather than defeated by the differences in your partner.

4. Determine that your effort to deal with your differences will reward you with a more varied, interesting, and fulfilling lifestyle than you would have achieved alone.

5. Make the most of attitudes, values, and preferences that you share and find active ways to express them together. Look for similarities underneath your differences; for example, one may be social while the other is private, but you may be able to enjoy a few close friends together.

6. Keep your differences working for you, not against you. Running a household or family requires a variety of interests, talents, and preferences. Don't compete; include. Your differences may be needed for well-rounded teamwork: one organizes, the other harmonizes; one fixes things, the other fixes people; one sees the big picture, the other the details; one brings the arts, the other sports; one brings sociability, the other solitude; one action, the other reflection; one thinks, the other feels.

Building compatibility is an ongoing, never-ending task. Family background and lifestyle preferences surrendered in the early years of marriage may resurface with renewed interest. The "differentness" in your partner that attracted you yesterday can become a problem tomorrow. Each stage of life and marriage presents a new challenge and a new opportunity.

10

Your Values Clash

Symptoms

You or your partner is disappointed and frustrated over differences that prevent the sharing of what is most important or enjoyable. Here are some examples:

One of you reads and fantasizes over *Better Homes and Gardens;* the other over travel magazines.

One of you tunes in football, the other a movie.

One of you watches TV, the other wants conversation.

One of you wants to purchase and care for a home of your own, the other wants freedom from mortgages and maintenance.

One of you is interested in charities or causes and wants to give time and money away; the other is concerned for comfort or security and wants to conserve resources.

Spiritual life and growth takes priority for one of you; religion is a bogus rip-off to the other.

Maintaining individuality and independence is important to one of you; the other prefers to share everything together.

One of you wants to take wings and wander; the other

wants to sprout roots and get established.

Having and nurturing children is important to one of you while the other wants freedom from family obligations.

One or both of you is increasingly disappointed that your partner does not share what is important to you. You may wish you were married to someone who did.

You or your partner may doubt at times that you want to share your life with someone with values and priorities so different from your own.

Diagnosis

Lives and marriages are built on a foundation of values.

Couples that share similar values readily pull in the same direction. They agree relatively easily about how to spend time, energy, and money. They can build a marriage, family, and life-style that feels right and comfortable to both with relatively little conflict.

Differences in values present a challenge to thinking and acting in harmony. Spouses often feel frustrated and dissatisfied when values pull them in opposite directions. When decisions become difficult, couples may not be aware that a difference in values is the source of the problem.

All couples hold some values in common—some more, some less. All couples experience conflict of values—some more, some less. Searching for a spouse with identical values is chasing a rainbow. Couples need to make the most of what they have in common and find mutually acceptable avenues for expressing what is not shared.

Values are often learned and ingrained early in life although some are held more firmly than others. A person may be able to change or alter one's own values with time and effort, but no one can change the values of another. Partners who attempt to pressure, nag, persuade, coerce, or seduce value changes in a spouse will experience frustration and defeat. Partners need to learn to live creatively with their differences rather than attempt to force uniformity.

Couples are often unaware of the values they each bring to their marriage that underlie their behavior, decisions, and conflicts. Spouses are sometimes surprised to discover important values in themselves that they might not consciously affirm. For example, a mate might affirm career goals as a top priority but invest more effort, energy, time, and money on reducing a golfing handicap. Or a spouse might affirm marriage and family as a priority, when behavior indicates that household decor is more important than the people who live there.

Clarifying individual values periodically can help couples understand and adjust to their similarities and differences. When values are held in common, interests are readily shared and enjoyed together. When values differ, separate activities can be accepted and affirmed. Exploring basic values can also help couples and individual spouses realign their commitments and activities with their real priorities.

Differences in values present a gift as well as a challenge. Partners with contrasting values stretch each other and help each other to learn and grow. The contrasting values of a spouse can bring balance and enrichment in areas where one's own are limiting.

Prescription

Get to know your own and your partners values so that you can build your marriage upon them—or around them.

Your values are not simply your stated ideals. In fact, your real values may differ sharply from what you believe them to be. Here are some questions that can help you identify and understand your values:

1. What was important to your family when you were growing up with respect to money, parenting, education, religion, neighbors, food, politics, recreation, marriage, family life, sex roles, housekeeping, and other areas of life that

seemed significant? Recall what parents and family actually seemed to feel and to do rather than what was said or taught.

2. When you were little, what did you think would be important to you when you grew up? What sort of lifestyle have your siblings or extended family (if any) chosen? What attracts or repels you about their choices?

3. On what sort of activities do you invest thought, energy, time, or money most easily? Look at your behavior as well as your ideals.

Such questions can expand your awareness of what is important to you so that you can compare your values with those of your partner. You are likely to discover—or rediscover—that you hold some priorities in common and differ on others. Identify the values that seem most important upon which you tend to agree and disagree.

As you discover what you hold in common, ask yourself whether your investment of time, energy, or money matches the values you share. You may discover that a fresh look at your shared priorities will lead you in new directions. For example, a clearer awareness of your shared values may redirect you to put more energy into building your relationship, going back to school, developing your spirituality, traveling, starting your own business, or buying a sailboat.

When your values conflict with those of your mate, search for underlying commonalities. For example, one may have a faith commitment while the other rejects religion altogether; yet you may share common causes and activities that address human needs.

Sometimes couples with differing values need to pursue them separately. You can understand and support each other also when you cannot act together. You need to talk about such differences, accept them as normal and inevitable, and let them keep you learning and growing.

Chapter 11

Introverts and Extroverts Marry

Symptoms

You and your partner relate to people in different ways. One or more of the following statements describe this difference.

One of you is energized being with people; the other becomes exhausted when socializing.

One of you is just beginning to enjoy a party when the other wants to go home.

One of you becomes lonely when others are not around; the other is more likely to feel lonely in a crowd.

One of you prefers the free-flowing chit-chat of informal social gatherings; the other prefers brief, structured events.

One of you gives priority to the social climate; the other to the physical environment.

One of you prefers a variety of relationships with many people; the other prefers a few, close friends.

One of you would like your home to be a social center; the other prefers a private retreat.

One of you thinks out loud, beginning a sentence without knowing how it will end; the other thinks and prepares before talking.

One of you discovers your emotions while expressing them; the other identifies emotions before expressing them.

One of you prefers to work and play with people; the other prefers to work and play with things and concepts.

Diagnosis

"Extrovert" and "introvert" are terms that describe personality types. Identified by Carl Jung, the famous Swiss psychiatrist, these types can help explain some of the inherent differences between people. Such differences when occurring between marriage partners can cause difficulties or bring rewards depending upon how couples respond to them.

"Extrovert" spouses tend to be sociable, oriented to the external world. Values and morals are shaped by their social consciousness. They prefer people to things and are receptive to a wide range of relationships. Social interaction is energizing. They work better with others than alone. They derive energy from social contact.

"Introvert" partners are more interested in projects or concepts than social relationships. Oriented to an internal world of ideas, they build values and morals based on inner conclusions. They find social interaction to be exhausting. They prefer a few close friends to larger social gatherings. They work better alone. They derive energy from inner processes. Home is a retreat from social obligation.

When "extroverts" and "introverts" marry. they can benefit from their "differentness" but need to accept and appreciate each others's unique qualities. "Introvert" partners can seem distant, withdrawn, almost antisocial at times. Their reluctance to invite or visit friends or to enjoy informal social events can bring loneliness and frustration to the "extrovert" mate. "Introverts" want to go home just when "extroverts" are beginning to enjoy a party. They often resist entertaining, preferring their home to be a private castle.

Nevertheless, the "extrovert" can profit from the "introvert" partner's inner consistency, steadiness, and depth of commitment. The "extrovert" can learn to enjoy a home that is protected and preserved as a retreat and to find security in a mate that is consistent, loyal, not easily swayed by changing circumstances or outside influences. If an "introvert" prefers to have only a few close friends, their spouse is likely to be the best one.

"Introverts" can also benefit from the gifts "extrovert" spouses bring to a relationship if they can understand and accept their differences. "Introverts" can be frustrated and irritated with the rambling, spontaneous, and seemingly endless conversations of "extroverts" who think while talking. They will often be pressured to socialize by their "extrovert" partners more than is desirable or comfortable. They may have difficulty maintaining privacy in their own home.

At the same time, "introverts" receive a variety of benefits from their "extrovert" spouses. Although they might be reluctant to participate, they benefit from the social contact their "extrovert" partners provide. "Extroverts" keep their mates in touch with what is going on in the lives of people around them—a reality to which they might otherwise be oblivious. "Extroverts" also bring energy, spontaneity, and liveliness to the home and family. Everyone needs at least one close friend, and, for the "introvert," that friend is likely to be the spouse.

Of course differences also cause problems. "Extroverts" and "introverts" often have difficulty communicating since one lives primarily in a world of external connections and the other of internal ideas. They face a challenge to build a lifestyle with the free-flowing sociability of an extrovert and the inwardness of an introvert.

Prescription

From the descriptions above, decide whether you are

inclined to be an "introvert" or an "extrovert." Then assess your partner and determine if this difference in type is an issue in your marriage.

If so, do not try to change your partner. "Introvert" and "extrovert" preferences are deeply ingrained and, although some stretching or modification may be possible, you will not be able to recreate your partner in your own image. Whatever alterations are possible will have to come at the initiative of your partner. You will only frustrate yourself and defeat your relationship with efforts to make your partner more like yourself.

You need to understand, accept, affirm, and appreciate the differences in your partner. Each of you contributes valuable personality qualities to your relationship. You can make your differences work for you.

If you are an "extrovert" with an "introvert" partner, you can benefit from the gifts your inwardly oriented spouse brings to your relationship. Here are some suggestions:

1. Think of the quiet depths of your partner as a gift of stability and strength.

2. Find security in your partner's inner loyalty and commitment.

3. Understand the effort, even exhaustion, that superficial socializing requires of your mate.

4. Understand that your spouse can be as lonely in a crowd as you can be when alone.

5. Find ways to satisfy your need for frequency and variety in social interaction elsewhere while nurturing a few close relationships to share with your spouse.

6. Don't interpret silence as boredom or withdrawal; your "introvert" spouse talks only after careful thought.

7. Learn to share your mate's love of home as a private retreat.

If you are an "introvert" with an "extrovert" partner, you, too, can benefit from your differences. Here are some suggestions:

1. Be aware of and appreciate the gift of social connectedness you receive through your mate.

2. Enjoy the energy that your spouse invests in your relationship.

3. Understand that your "extrovert" spouse becomes revitalized when socializing even as you become depleted.

4. Understand and accept your partner's need for human interaction and your limits in satisfying it.

5. Allow for a variety of social activities and relationships for your spouse that you prefer not to share.

6. Don't interpret or criticize your spouse's conversational rambling or inconsistencies as superficiality or stupidity; your "extrovert" spouse merely does mental processing outloud.

7. Learn to share your mate's love of home as a social center.

These suggestions can help you build the kind of teamwork that can keep your differences working for you and not against you.

Chapter 12

"Sensing" and "Intuiting" Types Marry

Symptoms

You and your partner are different in the way you enjoy life day by day and think about the future. This difference might be an issue in your marriage if one or more of the following statements apply.

One of you tends to be content to enjoy what each day brings while the other anticipates future changes.

One of you attends to household details while the other looks at the "big picture" and projects new possibilities for family living.

One of you enjoys food and lives to eat; the other merely satisfies hunger, eating to live. For example, when traveling, one looks for a unique, interesting restaurant; the other wants fast and convenient food.

One of you expresses your love with deeds; the others with words.

One of you wants to spend money to enjoy today; the other wants to invest to enjoy tomorrow.

For one of you, sex is as good as it feels to the senses; the other enjoys sexual relating with imagination and fantasy.

In conversation, one of you responds directly to what is said; the other often responds to suspected meanings or motives underlying what is actually stated.

One of you gives priority to the physical environment of your home such as furnishings and decor; the other gives priority to abstract qualities such as inner fulfillment. One changes furniture and wallpaper; the other changes lifestyle.

One shuns seemingly impractical or visionary schemes; the other shuns monotonous repetition.

Diagnosis

"Sensing" and "intuiting" are another set of contrasting personality traits identified by Carl Jung, the famous Swiss psychiatrist. When applied to couples, "sensing" partners tend to experience married life through their five senses: seeing, hearing, touching, smelling, and tasting. "Intuiting" spouses prefer to relate through an inner process of analysis. Marital partners with this "differentness" need to understand and accept it and to make it work for them and not against them.

"Sensing" spouses are practical, attentive to detail. While no one likes tedium, they are more tolerant of repetitious routine tasks than an "intuiting" partner. When life feels good, "sensing" spouses tend to be content. They are not restless for change. They live for today. They enjoy good food and attractive surroundings. They are excellent at attending to daily routines and bedtime rituals important to children. Sexual relating is enjoyed through the senses; sex is as good as it feels. "Sensing" spouses are practical and realistic, good at tending to details.

"Intuiting" spouses are imaginative. They see the big picture, not the details. They envision possibilities that would never occur to their "sensing" partners. They live for the future; today is only for getting ready for tomorrow. Thus they are often restless, and especially so when everyday life become repetitive. Processing reality inwardly, they may not be aware of the taste of their food, the decor of a room, or of new clothing worn by the spouse. "Intuiting" partners have little tolerance for routine details and feel oppressed by the more monotonous household or parenting tasks. Sexual relating has more to do with imagination or fantasy than with comfort or physical sensation. "Intuiting" partners like to share dreams and anticipate future changes but need someone else to tend to the practical details.

If you prefer "sensing" and have an "intuiting" spouse, your partner will not allow your life to bog down in ruts. You will be challenged by visions and possibilities that would never occur to you. You may sometimes feel anxious at those future plans of your "intuiting" partner that seem too risky or impractical. You may sometimes wish your partner were less restless, more content to enjoy the daily routines of your life together. You may be frustrated or resentful when your "intuiting" partner fails to notice new clothes, food, or furniture.

If you prefer "intuiting" and have a "sensing" spouse, you may be frustrated at your partner's lack of receptiveness to some of your dreams and ideas. Your partner is likely to prefer to spend resources on present enjoyment rather than future projections. While your restlessness for change can be threatening to your "sensing" partner, you open doors of possibilities your "sensing" partner would never even imagine. You have reason to be grateful for the contentment of your partner with everyday tasks; your partner tends to routine details you prefer to overlook.

"Sensing" and "intuiting" spouses need to value the gifts of the other and develop a balance between living today and enjoying tomorrow, between stability and change, between spending and investing, between commitment to larger life goals and attention to the tasks of each day.

"Sensing" and "intuiting" partners can help each other

grow. "Sensing" partners can learn to accept and enjoy the change and variety provided by an "intuiting" spouse. "Intuiting" partners can learn to enjoy the present moment which is, in fact, the only piece of time in which life can be lived.

"Sensing" and "intuiting" partners can make an effective and balanced team when working together. One sees the big picture, the other the details. One motivates with vision, the other attends to practical details. One plans the work, the other works the plan. Each needs the gifts of the other.

Prescription

From the descriptions above, determine if you are a "sensing" or "intuiting" type. Assess your partner's personality type and decide if this difference is an issue in your marriage.

Although your differences may prove frustrating at times, do not attempt to make alterations in your partner. You will not succeed. If you try to change your partner you will only defeat yourself and your relationship. Accept your differences so that you can appreciate what you each contribute.

Your "sensing-intuiting" difference presents you with both a challenge and an opportunity. You need to overcome the difficulties you are likely to have working side-by-side if only by agreeing at times to work separately. You can include both future dreams and routine daily events in your conversations. You can enjoy the benefits of filling the gaps for each other, one expanding horizons and the other tending to details. You can learn to celebrate your diversity of gifts that allow you to achieve together more than either of you could do alone.

If you prefer "sensing" and have an "intuiting" partner, the following can help you build compatibility out of your differences.

1. Learn to appreciate your "intuiting" spouse's ability to lift you out of familiar, comfortable routines into a future with more excitement and rewards than you would envision for yourself on your own.

2. Affirm your own unique gifts; keep remembering that your "intuiting" spouse needs your practicality, your attention to detail, and your enjoyment of the present.

3. Be careful not to blame yourself for your partner's restlessness or discontent. You do not cause it and you cannot change it.

4. Be aware that your efforts to please your partner are more likely to go unnoticed than unappreciated. Understanding your "intuiting" partner can help you to call attention without resentment to whatever deserves a compliment.

5. Do not allow yourself to feel threatened by future plans that seem impractical or overly risky. You can learn to enjoy your partner's vision of possibilities while you provide the constraints and balance of realism. You can talk of future dreams while still enjoying the pleasures of today. You can help your partner do the same.

If you prefer "intuiting" and have a "sensing" partner, the following can help you benefit from your differences.

1. Be aware that your "sensing" spouse's lack of enthusiasm for your aspirations is not a personal rejection but a result of a difference in personality type. Avoid creating undue anxiety when speculating about future plans with your partner. If your partner were less threatened, your excitement might become more contagious.

3. Listen thoughtfully to your partner's conversation about routine everyday events. These are as equally important as your own more generalized and speculative interests. You need to listen if you want to be heard.

4. Express your gratitude for your "sensing" spouse's realistic practicality. In fact, you need someone able to handle the routine, everyday rituals and details you find intolerable.

5. Compromise between spending for today and investing for tomorrow both for your own benefit as well as for your relationship. You can learn to enjoy today while you anticipate tomorrow. Your "sensing" spouse can enrich your life by helping you expand your awareness by making you take time to see the scenery, smell the roses, taste the coffee, feel the breeze, and hear the birds.

Whether you prefer "sensing" or "intuiting," you need to hold in memory the initial fascination you felt toward your partner. Very likely, your "differentness" helped make you attractive to each other. A "sensing" person can be attracted to the restless imagination of someone that prefers "intuiting." An "intuiting" person can be attracted to the practicality, contentment, and acceptance of everyday routine of a "sensing" mate. Don't let your disappointment with what is missing spoil your celebration of what you have.

Chapter 13
"Thinking" and "Feeling" Types Marry

Symptoms

One of you lives from the heart, the other from the head. One of you is a "people person" while the other lives in a more structured world. If one or more of the following statements describe your relationship, this may be an issue in your marriage. If so, this chapter is designed to help.

One of you is emotionally controlled while the other tends to be spontaneous.

When arguing, one of you is logical and analytical; the other is intuitive and emotional.

One of you is uncomfortable and defends against closeness; the other hungers for conversational and emotional intimacy.

One of you makes conversation that is brief and to the point; the other prefers conversation that is breezy and rambling.

One of you wants a well-organized and well-managed household; the other wants a home that is warm, relational, and harmonious.

When making a decision, one of you wants what is efficient or "correct"; the other wants what is pleasing to all involved.

When raising kids, one of you gives priority to order, discipline, and limits; the other to protection, caring, and nurture.

In your relationship, one of you prizes efficient cooperation; the other yearns for emotion and warmth.

When making love, one of you centers on the sex organs, moving efficiently toward orgasmic fulfillment; the other prefers a prolonged, total experience of the whole body, mind, and spirit.

Diagnosis

"Thinking" and "feeling" are another set of personality preferences identified by Carl Jung that can help explain differences between spouses. Of course, everyone both "thinks" and "feels," but individuals tend to base decisions primarily on one or the other.

The preference between "thinking" and "feeling" has nothing to do with competence. "Feeling" spouses may be more intelligent than "thinkers," but when making decisions they are more attentive to the feelings of people than to objective logic.

"Thinking" spouses tend to be logical, emotionally controlled, more comfortable with things than with people. They may appear to be insensitive at times, perhaps even cruel, when actually they are only analytical. They are more concerned to be logically correct than to do what pleases others. In fact, they may not be aware when they have offended their spouse. "Thinking" spouses provide the kind of security and stability that comes with emotional control and clear thinking under stress. They tend to be reliable, stable, and good providers. They help keep a household organized, planned, and efficient.

"Feeling" spouses tend to be spontaneous, expressive, and

socially comfortable. They are sensitive to feelings and base decisions largely on what pleases or displeases others. Warm and harmonious relationships are more important than efficiency or productivity. "Feeling" spouses provide sociability. They tend to be understanding, supportive, and nurturing. They need and enjoy higher levels of intimacy than "thinking" partners find comfortable. They bring energy and excitement to a relationship.

"Feeling" and "thinking" partners can defeat themselves and their relationship by trying to change each other into becoming more like themselves. "Thinking" partners are likely to want their spouses to be more analytical, more efficient, and to talk more to the point. They like to spend time alone with favorite projects. "Feeling" spouses are likely to want their partners to open up, share emotions, visit socially, and become more sensitive to feelings. Efforts to change a spouse are almost always futile. Some modifications in oneself may be possible with adequate motivation and effort, but no one is able to make significant personality changes in a partner.

"Thinking" and "feeling" people often find each other because each has something that benefits the other. "Thinking" spouses are attracted by the mate's energy and social interaction. For them, these provide a vicarious emotional outlet. "Feeling" spouses are attracted by the mate's emotional control, inner strength, practical competencies, and stability.

"Feeling" and "thinking" spouses can make an excellent team. Each has gifts the other lacks and together they fill each other's needs. One attends to things, the other attends to people. One provides organization and efficiency, the other warmth and harmony. One provides emotional control, the other emotional energy. One provides stability, the other spontaneity. One structures, the other nurtures. Both are needed, important and essential to a balanced team.

"Feeling" and "thinking" people need to understand, accept, and affirm their "differentness" in order to work as a team. Although this personality difference can cause problems later in marriage, it often attracted partners to each other in an early, more romantic stage. That first attraction was valid; different gifts enrich both partners. But such differences require understanding and effort when romance succumbs to reality.

Couples need to keep on appreciating each other's strengths rather than wallow in disappointment over what a spouse can never be. Capitalizing on the unique gifts of each partner, couples can enjoy a well-rounded, mutually satisfying, and rewarding teamwork.

Prescription

From the description above, determine if you tend more toward "thinking" or "feeling." Assess your partner's "type" as well. Decide if this difference is an issue in your marriage.

If you are a "thinking" "feeling" couple, you are faced with a challenge and an opportunity. You may have difficulty communicating. You may feel pressured, dissatisfied, inadequate, or lonely at times. You need to be thoughtful, accepting, and realistic about your relationship. An understanding of yourself and your partner will help.

If you are a "thinking" partner married to someone that prefers "feeling," here are some suggestions.

1. Keep in touch with your rewards for having a "feeling" spouse. Your spouse is probably your closest friend—possibly your only close friend.

2. Stretch yourself to share the social connections provided by your "feeling" partner. Without them, you would be out of touch with the people around you.

3. Expand your tolerance of free flowing, breezy conversa-

tion which may seem pointless to you but is essential to your partner.

4. Understand the deep and pressing need behind your "feeling" partner's invitation to open up and express your feelings even though it may seem impossible for you to respond. Not knowing what is going on inside of you, makes your partner feel lonely and isolated. Though you may not find it easy, you have a great deal to gain by making an effort to share your inner world.

5. Accept the fact that you will probably not be able to satisfy your "feeling" partner's relational needs for close personal relating.

6. Encourage your partner to build a circle of appropriate relationships outside of your marriage that satisfy these needs. Do not allow yourself to become jealous of these outside relationships; they work for you, not against you. They meet important needs in your partner you are not able to satisfy.

7. Stretch yourself increasingly to tolerate higher levels of conversational, emotional, physical, and sexual intimacy. You will benefit together with your marriage.

If you are a "feeling" partner married to a "thinking" spouse, here are some suggestions that can help you make it work:

1. Keep remembering your initial romantic attraction to your "thinking" spouse. Rekindle your appreciation for the inner strength and emotional control of the "strong silent" type.

2. Keep in touch with the practical advantages of having a "thinking" spouse. Your partner is likely to provide stability, security, and problem-solving resources. Your energy needs organization. Your spontaneity needs direction. Your emotion needs reflection.

3. Do not expect your partner to satisfy all your relational needs. Don't allow unrealistic expectations to keep you dissatisfied. One person cannot meet all your social needs, especially not your "thinking" partner.

4. Satisfy unmet relational needs outside of marriage in appropriate and acceptable ways without feeling resentment toward your partner. Do not allow yourself to become overly "needy" and demanding with your "thinking" partner.

5. Understand your partner's reserved emotional distance as a personality trait, not a personal rejection.

6. Keep reminding yourself that your "thinking" partner means well even when hurtful and apparently insensitive. Your spouse probably cares for you a great deal but only lacks an awareness of your feelings.

7. Express appreciation frequently for the gifts and strengths of your partner which meet other, nonsocial but important needs. Your "thinking" partner is most likely to open up when feeling unpressured, accepted, and appreciated.

You were probably attracted to each other partly because of your personality differences. Don't spoil it by trying to remake your partner to be like yourself. Keep appreciating and respecting your differences. Make them work for you and not against you.

Chapter 14

"Judging" and "Perceiving" Types Marry

Symptoms

One of you wants a world of structure and order; the other prefers a flexible world with a variety of alternatives. If this is an issue in your relationship, one or more of the following statements will apply.

One of you wants a matter decided, the other wants to keep options open.

A decision settles a matter for one of you, the other feels free to ignore or change decisions.

One of you wants the security of advanced planning, the other wants the freedom of flexibility. For example, when traveling together, one wants to make plans and reservations in advance to avoid uncertainty or disappointment; the other likes to keep choices open to take advantage of unfolding possibilities.

One of you holds relatively fixed opinions and positions on most topics and issues under discussion; the other reflects on the data without arriving at firm conclusions. Conversations tend to be too inconclusive for one, too opinionated for the other.

One of you wants to share a life that is well-ordered with everything in its place; the other prefers a life full of variety and change.

One of you wants predictability; the other prefers an open future.

One of you finds the lack of mutually held opinions to be frustrating and nonsupportive; the other experiences the pressure to share fixed opinions to be oppressively confining.

Diagnosis

Carl Jung labeled the contrasting personality types described above as "judging" and "perceiving."

Spouses that prefer "judging" over "perceiving" are most comfortable when decisions are made and consistently followed. They do not like loose ends. They like to come to conclusions and tend to have fixed opinions on most subjects. They may alter an opinion, but they are not comfortable with indecision. They tend to express themselves in strong, absolute terms. Spouses who do not share their conclusions seem unsupportive and, perhaps, a bit disloyal. A partner's ongoing openness and indecision can add to the kind of disorder and chaos they dislike.

Spouses that prefer "perceiving" over "judging" like to keep options open. They tend to be uncomfortable with fixed plans, firm opinions, or final decisions. They resist attempts to pin them down. They postpone decisions preferring to seek more information. Even when a decision seems to have been made, they are still exploring additional alternatives. They are inquisitive, receptive, reluctant to close doors to future possibilities. They avoid committing to a plan or making inflexible decisions. They feel confined and oppressed by a spouse that demands decisions, conclusions, or firm commitments.

Communication often breaks down between "perceiving"

and "judging" spouses. "Judging" partners tend to feel frustrated and unsupported when conversing with a "perceiving" mate that responds to an opinion with curiosity rather than agreement. "Judging" partners yearn for the bonding that comes with shared convictions; their "perceiving" mates enjoy the stimulation of mutual exploration. The probing questions of the "perceiving" partner can seem like negative criticism to the "judging" spouse; the firm opinions of the "judging" spouse can seem like a straitjacket to the "perceiving" mate.

In spite of these differences, if "judging" and "perceiving" partners understand, accept, affirm, and appreciate their differences, they make a balanced and productive team. The "judging" spouse provides structure and planning and sees that necessary decisions are made and implemented. The "perceiving" partner keeps life flexible, expands options, allows for growth and spontaneity, and responds fluidly to new opportunities.

How and when such personality differences are determined is not known. These characteristics appear early in childhood and are reinforced by life experiences. Although some modification may be possible, each spouse's basic orientation does not significantly change.

Prescription

From the descriptions above, determine if you have a "perceiving" or a "judging" preference. Assess your partner's type. Determine if this "differentness" is an issue in your relationship.

Is so, do not attempt to change your partner to become more like yourself. You can't do it. Any attempt will result in frustration and resentment.

Accept, affirm, and appreciate your differences as a gift. The more positive your response to the "differentness" of your partner, the better you will be able to make it work for you and for your marriage.

Your "differentness" presents a challenge to your conversation, especially when it comes to making decisions. The greater your personality difference, the more effort you need to invest in building bridges of affirmation and understanding. On the positive side, the more your "differentness," the greater the benefit.

If you have a "judging" preference and a "perceiving" spouse, the indecisive, noncommittal, open-endedness of your partner is likely to present a challenge to your patience and understanding. You are likely to resent your partner's apparent lack of cooperation and support. You do not get the affirmation you want and need. Long and tiring discussions fail to arrive at clear shared commitment. The following suggestions can help:

1. Remind yourself that your partner's apparent lack of commitment and support is not a personal rejection but a personality trait.

2. Stretch your capacity to live with ambiguity, unanswered questions, flexibility, and indecision. Allow for new options, fresh ideas, and surprises. More than one answer can be right; there is more than one way to do anything. You may find that some decisions and plans work best when left open as long as possible.

3. Press yourself to shift more responsibility for planning and decisions to your spouse even when you are anxious about the results. Your partner is probably more responsible than you think and will come through if you can let go.

4. Do not expect your partner to support your convictions without reservations no matter how important to you at the moment. You will only be disappointed if you do. Do not interpret a lack of commitment to your position as a betrayal or lack of personal affirmation.

If you have a "perceiving" preference and a "judging"

partner, you are likely to find the fixed opinions and conclusions of your spouse confining, perhaps even oppressive.
You resent pressures to agree with opinions or decisions
you are not ready to accept. You feel unnecessarily limited
by firm plans that do not take all the options into considera-
tion. Here are some suggestions that can help you with
these differences:

1. Remind yourself that your spouse's need for fixed
opinions and decisions is a personality trait and not an effort
to limit, confine, or control you.

2. Stretch yourself to enjoy the relaxing predictability that
comes with firm plans and decisions.

3. Reassure your "judging" spouse by becoming more
specific about how you will handle your responsibility. Do
not shrug off as unimportant your partner's interest in
details. Your partner will be better able to tolerate indecision
when the options are clear and your procedure is specific.

4. Be open to discover paradoxically that sometimes freedom and flexibility can expand when routine decisions and
responsibilities are handled with dispatch.

Whether you prefer "perceiving" or "judging," your challenge is to understand, appreciate, affirm, and celebrate the
unique gifts you each bring to your relationship and to keep
your "differentness" working for you and not against you.

Chapter 15

You Need Personal Support

Symptoms

You or your partner needs more affirmation, understanding, acceptance, and support. If this is an issue for your relationship, one or more of the following will apply.

One or both of you . . .

. . . feels a lack of confidence and affirmation from your partner when taking risks in a new venture such as building a career, going back to school, or starting a business.

. . . feels neglected when you are sick or worried about your health.

. . . feels that your partner does not really care when you are disappointed as, for example, when you are passed over for a promotion, neglected by a friend, or having difficulty at work or school.

. . . feels that your partner does not try to understand when you are grieving as, for example, when you have lost something or someone important to you.

. . . feels that your partner does not really listen when you are hurt and angry.

. . . does not feel that your partner has confidence in your judgment and ability when you are faced with a difficult situation or decision.

. . . yearns for more acceptance and understanding of your feelings from your partner.

Diagnosis

Although perhaps somewhat exaggerated, the descriptions above indicate a breakdown in giving and receiving the kind of personal support most spouses expect from their mate. Serious marital dissatisfaction is likely to develop if either spouse fails to receive appropriate emotional support from a partner, especially at critical times. At the same time, many partners have difficulty asking for, receiving, or giving the kind of support that is needed in a specific situation.

Everyone needs a support network. The care, protection, understanding, and nurture of parents (or surrogates) is essential to life in childhood. Grown-ups give and receive emotional support differently but they never outgrow their need for it.

The desire and need for emotional support is probably stronger than most partners realize. Few people get married for the expressed purpose of finding emotional support. And few people express a lack of such support as a reason for ending a marriage. Nevertheless, the lack of emotional support is a major source of marital failure.

Extramarital affairs, particularly those most serious and destructive to a marriage, are often established more for emotional support than for sexual gratification. The explanation is familiar: "She understands me." "He listens to me."

No one can completely satisfy the need for emotional support from marriage alone. Efforts to do so can suffocate a relationship. Expecting a mate to meet all emotional support needs imposes an impossible burden. Everyone needs a network of caring people to catch them like a safety net when they seem to be losing their grip. Friends, family, neighbors, associates at work, colleagues, etc. are needed in addition to spouses. If a mate is unable or unwilling to respond to a need, others can fill in.

At the same time, for most couples, the spouse needs to be the main source of support. If almost all personal support is found elsewhere, a marriage is likely to grow distant and irrelevant. Perhaps for most successful couples about 50 percent of support needs are satisfied by a spouse and 50 percent outside of marriage. That kind of split is, of course, arbitrary and changes with individuals and situations.

Both partners need to give and receive emotional support. If one partner does all the giving and the other all the receiving, an unstable, and probably unhealthy, dependency is likely to develop. We all have dependency needs and we all have the capacity to meet these needs for others. Couples need to give and receive in balance.

Prescription

Accept your own and your partner's need for emotional support as normal and appropriate.

Avoid extremes of overdependence and independence. Don't drain or suffocate your mate with continual demands for supportive attention. Don't deprive yourself or distance your partner with an exaggerated independence.

Take responsibility for your own support needs. Tell your partner what you want and need. Don't expect your partner to read your mind or interpret your mood. Don't take the attitude: "If I have to ask, it doesn't count." That attitude will keep both you and your partner frustrated and dissatisfied.

Make it your goal to understand your partner's need for emotional support and to respond appropriately. When in doubt, ask what would be helpful. Do not assume that your partner wants the same type of responses that feel good to you.

Chapter 16

Emotional Support Doesn't Help

Symptoms

Sometimes well-meaning responses to a hurting partner do not help. Here are some examples.

One of you is disappointed, troubled, sick, anxious, hurting or angry; the other wants to be helpful, but actually makes it worse by responses such as . . .

. . . "How did you get yourself into this?"

. . . "Cheer up, it's really not so bad; you'll soon feel better."

. . . "You think you have it bad? Let me tell you what happened to me. . ."

. . . "Here is what you should do . . . ."

. . . "You shouldn't feel that way . . . ."

. . . "Come on, now, give me a smile . . . ."

. . . "Okay, tell me your problem and I'll see what I can do."

If this is the way you respond to a hurting spouse, you may be puzzled that your partner does not appreciate your efforts. You sincerely want to help but you only seem to make matters worse.

If your partner reacts this way to you when you are hurting, you may decide to hide your fears and hurts because such responses make you feel more vulnerable, anxious, confused, or incompetent. You yearn for a partner that listens, understands, cares, affirms, accepts, and believes in you.

Diagnosis

Reactions to a hurting spouse such as those described above often come from mates who genuinely care and want to help. But good intentions are not enough. Such responses can increase anxiety, reduce self-confidence, and add to the pain of a hurting mate.

Many spouses feel inadequate when responding to a hurting partner. They want to help, but their best efforts frustrate and alienate. They need to know what helps and what doesn't.

Helpful responses to an anxious or hurting partner usually convey *understanding, acceptance,* and *affirmation*. These can be expressed in words, gestures, actions, or touching.

Responses that convey *understanding* include attentive listening, genuine caring, and an effort to reflect an awareness of the partner's feelings. Helpful responses tend to invite the partner to express or explore feelings. Accurate empathy is the goal. Examples of unhelpful responses that hinder understanding might include a glib assurance that you "know how it feels," shifting attention to yourself by focusing on similar feelings of your own, efforts to cheer up the partner or an ignoring of feelings by focusing on the facts.

Responses that convey *acceptance* reassure a vulnerable partner that weaknesses and "negative" emotions can be safely expressed without fear of criticism or judgment. The need for nurturance is accepted as normal and healthy also in mates that seem strong and competent. Examples of unhelpful, judgmental responses might include a subtle blaming for being in the situation, the suggestion that an emotion expressed is inappropriate, or an inference that deeper pathology may underlie the current problem.

Responses that convey *affirmation* come from the confidence that the partner is competent and resourceful. The best gift spouses can give is not to share their own resources but to surface and affirm the partner's competence. Affirming a hurting spouse includes conveying confidence in your partner's ability to think, to solve problems, and to handle the current problem competently. Examples of unhelpful, nonaffirming responses might include an effort to think for the partner, to try to "fix" the problem (as if the spouse were not up to the task), or to suggest, however subtly, that the partner is inadequate to cope.

Words are not always the best supportive response for hurting partners. Thoughtful attentiveness, listening, touching, holding, stroking, massaging, or snuggling may be more helpful than words for some spouses in some situations.

Partners need to know what they want from each other when in need of emotional support. They also need to know what is most helpful to their hurting mates. Unfortunately, most couples rarely or never talk about these needs or ask for what is wanted.

Prescription

Make it your responsibility to get the kind of support you need. Do not expect your partner to guess how you feel and what you want. Let yourself know exactly what you want and then let it be okay to ask for it. Don't expect more than your partner can give. Find the emotional support that your spouse is unable to provide from other appropriate sources such as extended family, close friends, and nurturing organizations.

Make it your goal to understand the kind of emotional support that is most helpful to your spouse. Learn how to respond when your spouse is down, depressed, disappointed, sick, anxious, upset, angry, or whatever. Don't assume that your mate wants the same responses you prefer. For example, when sick, you might want active attention while your spouse prefers to be left alone.

Although not every spouse wants the same kind of emotional support, some responses seem helpful to almost everyone. Here are basic helping skills you can use:

1. *Convey understanding.* Let your first task be a genuine effort to listen attentively and reflect understanding. Eye contact and focused body posture when appropriate can help. Listening is almost always more helpful than talking. Limit your first responses to reflecting feelings, clarifying, and empathizing.

2. *Convey nonjudgmental acceptance.* Your partner needs a climate free from blame or criticism in order to be free to express thoughts and feelings openly and to ask for emotional support. Firmly resist every inner temptation to evaluate the appropriateness of your mate's feelings or behavior. Fight any inclination to assess the situation by assigning blame. A judgmental response, however subtle, is likely to result in guarded or hidden feelings and a search for a safer, more accepting source of support.

3. *Convey affirmation.* You are most likely to be helpful to a hurting partner when you show confidence in your spouse's own ability to cope, think, and handle the situation. Do not treat your partner as overly fragile, incompetent, unable to think for self, or to cope effectively with life situations. Discounting the competence of a partner is destructive although it is often well-intended. Avoid every temptation to think, decide, solve problems, or try to "fix" anything for your partner. Respond with the confidence that your partner will be competent to cope after working through the anxiety, fear, anger, sadness, or pain.

Do not limit your responses to the kinds of support with

which you are familiar or that you might prefer to offer. Other responses might be more helpful to your mate. Three kinds of responses that convey understanding, acceptance, and affirmation include:

Touching. You and your partner probably have favorite ways you like to be touched based on early childhood experiences. Some like to be stroked on the forehead, hair, back, feet, etc. Some like being hugged, head held on lap, holding hands, cuddling, etc. You need to let your partner know what feels good to you when you are hurting. You need to know what kind of touching feels best to your partner.

Empathy. This requires both the ability to sense the feelings underneath the words of your hurting partner and to convey your understanding. This needs to be done without evaluation or criticism. Sample responses: "That really hurts." "I can see how scary that can be." "How very sad." Or, in a positive situation, "That's exciting." When feelings are not obvious, you may need to explore or check out your assumptions in a manner that is inviting and not accusing: "You look sad, but sound angry."

Thoughtful actions. You can express caring both with words and actions. Take care not to assume you know what your partner wants. Better to ask than to guess. "Would you like me to stay with you? to fix you something? to hold you (see above)? to take care of the kids? to make your phone calls?" etc.

Such responses may seem strange, artificial, and difficult especially if you experienced limited nurturing as a child. You may be uncomfortable giving or receiving emotional support as an adult. You may need to stretch yourself to live with the discomfort you feel with such responses until they become natural. Another section addresses problems in giving or receiving emotional support.

Learning to give genuinely helpful supportive responses is one of the best gifts you can give to your marriage.

Chapter 17
Emotional Support Is Difficult to Give

Symptoms

One of you is upset, down, anxious, or hurting and the other . . .

. . . seems unaware of these feelings.

. . . withdraws, feeling inadequate or incompetent to help.

. . . resents the partner's apparent "weakness."

. . . withholds support fearful of reinforcing an unhealthy dependency.

. . . refuses support in fear that the partner's need is insatiable.

. . . denies support in retaliation for the partner's failure to provide emotional support.

. . . responds with a counterclaim for emotional support.

If you are the partner that is unable or unwilling to provide emotional support, you may be aware of a growing disappointment and discontent in the spouse.

If you are the partner whose need for emotional support is unsatisfied, you may feel unloved, uncared for, and dissatisfied with the marriage.

Diagnosis

A failure to provide emotional support when wanted and needed often results in serious marital dissatisfaction. Yet many spouses fail to reach out or respond helpfully to a hurting mate.

Inner blocks to giving effective emotional support often begin in childhood. Spouses that experienced little nurturing as a child may lack an adequate inner model for giving emotional support as adults. Some who were not allowed to show "weakness" as a child may not tolerate vulnerability in spouse. Some who experienced a pathologically dependent relationship in the past may be fearful of creating a similar trap by responding to dependency needs in the present.

Some spouses are blocked by resentfulness at what appears to be weakness in their spouse. They tend to see the spouse as a provider or protector and become anxious and angry at an appearance of inadequacy. Although they may not be aware of their dependency, they may rely on the spouse as a child depends on a parent to be strong, in control, on top of every situation. Such a difficult and unrealistic demand can blind a spouse to the emotional needs of a partner and block the willingness to respond.

Some spouses are blocked by a fear that responding to dependency needs in a partner will result in a "bottomless pit" which can never be filled to satisfaction. An underlying sense of awkwardness or inadequacy when providing emotional support can reinforce such a fear. They may define dependency needs as abnormal, and, in fact, may have been misused or abused in the past by someone with a pathological dependency. They withhold emotional support as a defense, hoping, perhaps, that if the need is not met, it will go away. This would be similar to refusing to feed a hungry child in hope that by not eating it will overcome its need for food.

Some spouses are blocked whenever they deal with emotions, especially vulnerable ones such as fear or sadness. They may be willing to define, analyze, and seek solutions to problems on a cognitive level, but they shy away from the closeness of emotional support. Their problem-solving skills can be helpful but only after emotional needs are satisfied.

Blocks preventing the giving of emotional support can be defeating to spouses individually and can result in serious marital dissatisfaction.

Prescription

You can learn to provide at least some of the emotional support your spouse wants and needs. Everyone can. However, you may need to stretch and grow as you learn to do it.

Do not allow feelings of inadequacy convince you that you lack the capacity to provide emotional support. You received sufficient nurturing as a child to sustain life. The nurturing you received in childhood is a permanent part of your personality and is a resource for providing emotional support as an adult. You have the capacity to give in the present what you have received in the past although you may not be aware of it. You may need to stretch yourself to try new and uncomfortable behaviors in order to recover nurturing responses buried within. All areas of your life in addition to your marriage will benefit if you do.

Identify your inner attitudes that get in the way of supportive responses. For example, be aware of any tendency to define the need for emotional support in your mate as immature, unnatural, or unhealthy. Adults never outgrow the need for security, protection, understanding, holding, or stroking especially when anxious, depressed, or hurting. Tell yourself that emotional support is as essential to your partner as food, shelter, clothing, or medical care.

Be alert to competitive patterns that undermine emotional support. You and your partner may want and expect affirmation, understanding, or appreciation at the same time. Each of you may feel convinced that your own need is more urgent or deserving. Be aware of such competition. You will not get what you want and need unless your partner's needs are satisfied as well. You both win or you both lose. Talk about it. Find cooperative ways for giving and receiving that satisfy both of you.

You may be blocked from giving emotional support by an underlying fear that your partner would become "insatiable." You need to test this against reality. The solution is not to withhold emotional support but to respond appropriately while at the same time taking care of your own needs. Your withholding may contribute to an escalating urgency in your partner's demands.

If you are blocked from responding to your hurting partner because you cannot tolerate seeing your spouse "weak" or vulnerable, test your fears against reality. You may be inappropriately transferring past expectations of parents to your mate. You may feel inadequate to take care of yourself and thus frightened and angry when your partner does not appear sufficiently strong to take care of you. You need to know that strong and competent people also have dependency needs. Your partner is actually stronger when such needs are expressed and satisfied. Providing appropriate emotional support to your mate increases strength and competence and thus adds to your security.

Accepting your own and your partner's need for emotional support is a sign of maturity in a relationship. Of course, such support must flow both ways. Be careful not to become competitive over who gives and who receives most. Don't keep score. You can discover patterns of giving and receiving that make winners of you both.

Chapter 18

Emotional Support Is Difficult to Receive

Symptoms:

You or your partner has difficulty reaching out and asking for emotional support or receiving what is offered. One or more of the following descriptive statements will apply if this is an issue in your relationship.

One or both of you . . .

. . . hides your need for support behind a facade of self-sufficiency.

. . . is afraid to reach out for emotional support for fear of disappointment or rejection.

. . . hides your need and desire for emotional support because you are reluctant to open up your inner world of thoughts and feelings.

. . . refuses to reach out and ask for emotional support convinced that if your partner really cared, you would not need to ask.

. . . is reluctant to reveal that you are down or hurting for fear of being blamed.

. . . is afraid to reach out for emotional support for fear of appearing childish.

. . . is reluctant to reach out for emotional support in fear of becoming overly dependent or controlled.

. . . looks for a flaw in the partner's effort to respond to your emotional needs, perhaps preferring to be angry than to feel vulnerable.

. . . hides your need and desire for emotional support from yourself as well as from your partner.

Diagnosis

Reaching out for and receiving emotional support is difficult for some spouses. Even though their partners may be able and willing to respond helpfully, their needs go unsatisfied.

Inner attitudes or blocks with roots in childhood can get in the way of reaching out for emotional support. Spouses perpetuate patterns learned from parents or significant siblings. Some families react to a sad, anxious, or hurting child with "smother" love that is over-controlling and under-affirming. Some families react with blame or criticism. Some react to pain with humor or even ridicule, adding injury to insult. Some families, intolerant of anything that seems like weakness, respond with demands to "grow up," "stop blubbering," and to act tough. Dysfunctional families may not respond to a hurting child at all. Spouses that grow up in such families learn to hide their need for emotional support from themselves and their partners rather than risk disappointment, hurt, or rejection.

Such childhood experiences get in the way of feeling or expressing vulnerable emotions such as anxiety or sadness. Thus some partners will get angry rather than appear weak or childish. They may, for example, angrily point out flaws in every effort to support them. Although unaware of the choice, they prefer to feel angry than vulnerable. Anger preserves a sense of strength and control. Thus efforts to provide support are rejected, the supportive partner is frustrated, and the hurting spouse stews in isolation. Nobody wins.

Some spouses close their eyes to emotional needs. They think rather than feel. They try to "fix" things quickly so the feelings will go away. They define, analyze, and explore alternative solutions rather than reach out for warmth or understanding. Although they appear to rise above their pain, never asking for emotional support and declining what is offered, nevertheless they often yearn inwardly for what they have learned to do without.

Unrealistic romantic expectations or a yearning from childhood for a responsive parent can also block receiving emotional support. Some hurting spouses refuse to ask for the support they need because they want their partner to know what they want and to respond without being asked. Their protests are familiar: "If my partner really loved me, I wouldn't have to ask." Or, more angrily, to the mate, "If you don't know what I want, I'm certainly not going to tell you!"

Such expectations rarely work out in real life. Although married partners often understand each other in depth, they remain separate persons with individual and changing needs. Couples never outgrow the need to tell each other what they need in a specific situation. Mind-reading does not come with a marriage license.

Inability or resistance to receiving emotional support for whatever reason is self-defeating, frustrating to a partner, and reduces marital satisfaction.

Prescription

You can overcome your barriers to reaching out for or accepting emotional support but you may need to stretch and grow.

You received and accepted nurturing when you were a small child and you can recover your ability to accept it as an adult. Someone held, clothed, fed, and responded to your emotional needs when you were little or you would not be alive. You have a child inside that still has such needs and that can relearn to accept and receive emotional support.

Determine to take some risks. Try some new behavior. Don't allow yourself to be imprisoned in behavior patterns that do not satisfy your needs. Do not assume that your partner will think less of you or discount your competence if you allow yourself to be vulnerable. Do not assume that your partner will criticize or blame you as your own family might have done. Your mate is not likely to laugh at you in your pain as siblings often do. Do not expect your partner to know exactly what you want or need. Help your partner to respond appropriately.

Trust your partner. Allow yourself to be "weak" or vulnerable with your mate. Dependency feelings are normal and healthy. You do not always have to be strong, controlled, or self-sufficient. If showing "weakness" threatens your partner, challenge your partner to grow.

Resist blaming your partner when your needs are unsatisfied. Take responsibility for getting what you want. Help your partner to understand your needs. Tell your partner what helps and what doesn't.

Don't expect too much from your partner. Your partner is not your only source of emotional support. Make the most of the support your partner is able and willing to provide but look elsewhere when more is needed. Find among your family, friends, associates, and neighbors individuals that can respond helpfully to your support needs.

Don't look for flaws in your partner's efforts to respond to you or allow yourself to become resentful when dissatisfied. Anger may help you maintain an illusion of strength and control, but it will not get you the emotional support you need. Affirm your partner's efforts to support you, make the best use of what is offered, and let your mate know how to become more helpful.

Resist the temptation to "fix" it quickly to avoid uncomfortable emotions. You can define, analyze, and problem-solve later after you have allowed yourself to be understood and supported in your sadness, anxiety, disappointment, or pain. Practical solutions work best after emotional needs are satisfied.

Resist making unrealistic expectations of your partner. Do not expect your partner to know what you want without asking. Your partner cannot read your mind. Do not discount what your partner gives because you had to ask. Take added satisfaction in helping your partner meet your needs. With your help, your partner can enjoy giving as much as you benefit from receiving. You both win.

Do not allow one partner to do the giving while the other receives. Both partners need to both give and receive. But do not keep score. It does not need to be fair; it only needs to work. Freely receive, freely give.

Chapter 19

When Marriage Stunts Growth

Symptoms

While one of you is growing or changing, the other responds with deprecating humor, sarcasm, or comments that tend to undermine confidence and self-esteem. If this occurs in your relationship, one or more of the following is likely to apply:

One or both of you . . .

. . . tends to notice and spotlight weaknesses, inconsistencies, or flaws in your partner.

. . . mimics, imitates, caricatures, or finds other ways to get laughs at the partner's expense.

. . . takes delight in exposing the embarrassment of the partner.

. . . frequently refers to your partner's behavior as clumsy, stupid, or inept—though perhaps under the guise of a joke.

. . . defends such criticism by innocently insisting: "I'm only kidding," or "Can't you take a joke?"

. . . hides embarrassment or faults from your partner for fear of ridicule.

. . . feels less intelligent, competent, or attractive in the presence of your partner than with other people.

. . . may laugh like a good sport at the partner's cutting humor while inwardly feeling hurt and resentful.

. . . feels increasingly anxious or incompetent because of the self-doubt or insecurity instilled by the partner.

Diagnosis

Ideally, married partners provide the encouragement and affirmation that enables both partners to develop toward their potential. Partners have a need and a right to expect their mates to believe in them, to want them to grow, and to provide the kind of support needed day-by-day to become their best selves.

Partners need one another to help build and sustain a positive self-image. The need for such support becomes pressing when a partner is making significant changes such as returning to school, starting a business, or launching a new career. At such times, spouses have a right to expect the kind of affirmation and support from their mates that builds confidence.

Competition, fear of abandonment, resistance to change, rigid relational roles, and other blocks to sensitivity often prevent couples from providing the kind of affirmation that allows for change and growth. Instead of loving each other into becoming their best selves, spouses often imprison each other in self-doubt or even self-loathing.

Belittling humor can reinforce a negative self-image. Highlighting flaws or weaknesses tends to reinforce them and undermine self-confidence. A lack of support combined with undermining responses can block or impede the growth of a spouse.

A significant change in the life of either partner often results in a crisis in the marriage. A venturing spouse needs additional understanding and affirmation. Spouses who have difficulty accepting changes are likely to discount, disparage, or even ridicule the competence of their anxious and vulnerable partners at a time when support is most needed. Marriages sometime break when caught in this tension.

Spouses making changes that threaten their partners need to see beyond their own need for support to understand the anxious resistance of their mates. Building up a partner is not easy when feeling needy, vulnerable, or uncertain yourself. Yet both tasks are needed to sustain a relationship while making significant changes.

Spouses that highlight flaws and weaknesses with humor may not intend to hurt. They are often unaware of the damage done to a spouse's self-image. They may have a keen sense of humor and genuinely want the partner to share in a laugh. "Can't you take a joke?" "Where is your sense of humor?" they plead righteously to the partner's pain. This puts the partner in a bind: how can one defend against a humorous put-down while everyone is laughing and not appear to lack a sense of humor?

Laughter, of course, is healthy and can be healing. A sense of humor is a gift to a relationship. Occasionally, laughter derived from the foibles of a spouse might clear the air and bring perspective, especially when the partner has a strong, positive self-image.

But humor can cut painfully. A steady diet of humorous put-downs can do long-term damage to the self-image. Many spouses understandably bail out of a confidence-destroying relationship in search of a more nurturing, affirming partner.

Highlighting the weaknesses of others with humor is often learned in childhood. Points are won in siblings rivalry more by spotlighting the flaw in others than by lifting up one's own achievements. Belittling others can become a family pattern and a way of life. Married partners often repeat sibling rivalry with each other. Spouses who feel vaguely superior when laughing at the mate's expense may be caught up in such competition.

Spouses whose humor and habits tend to put the partner down may have difficulty giving affirmation. Expressing support directly might seem artificial, unauthentic, or unsophisticated. In fact, if affirmation is not genuine, it will not be helpful. At the same time, some spouses cling to a lifelong illusion that their partners genuinely enjoy being put-down by their cleverness and wit when actually it only causes pain.

Everyone needs a steady diet of acceptance, affirmation, and appreciation in order to develop and grow. The best gift you can give a spouse is not to impart your own wit or wisdom but to draw out and affirm the competence of the mate.

Prescription

You and your partner are probably more important to each other's self-image than you realize. You can be an asset or a liability. If you want a healthy marriage and a healthy partner, provide the kind of affirmation and support needed for growth and development.

Be aware that you cannot avoid giving feedback to each other. Your comments, jokes, observations, or attitudes toward your partner will build confidence and reinforce a positive self-esteem or tear it down.

If you particularly enjoy humor based on your partner's flaws, weaknesses, or miscues, determine to give three or more affirmations for each put-down. As an alternative, you could make yourself the brunt of your jokes.

Your partner needs to be affirmed as intelligent, attractive, competent, and lovable. Target your affirmations at the points where your partner feels least confident or most vulnerable, probably the same weaknesses you have highlighted with humor. For example, if your partner feels or acts confused at times, compliment good thinking at every opportunity.

Appreciate and celebrate growth and development in your

partner. If you feel uncomfortable with positive changes in your partner, you may be caught up in competition, fear of abandonment, or resistance to change in ways that undermine your marriage. Determine not to allow your rivalry or anxieties to prevent you from providing the kind of support your partner needs. Provide affirmation when and how it is needed, not merely as you are inclined to give it.

Do not assume that affirming your partner's growth or development will come naturally. Support is often most difficult to give when most needed.

Support your mate even when you feel vulnerable yourself. If you are the one making personal or professional changes that are undesirable or threatening to your partner, you need to be patient, understanding, and realistic in your expectations of support. You are more likely to receive the affirmation you need if you show understanding for your partner's resistance. Once again, as noted, support is often most needed when most difficult to provide.

You can learn to find real satisfaction and fulfillment in the growth and development of your partner. In any case, you cannot win by making your partner a loser.

Don't let your marriage stunt your partner's growth. Don't let it stunt your growth. Instead, love each other into becoming your best selves.

Chapter 20

Emotional Support Is Confused with Sex

Symptoms

When the need for emotional support gets a sexual response, neither sex nor nurture is likely to be satisfying. This could be an issue in your relationship if one or more of the following statements apply.

One or both of you . . .

. . . reaches out for nurturing when you actually want sex.

. . . comes on sexually when you actually want to be held supportively.

. . . gives mixed signals so that your partner is unclear whether you want sex or emotional support.

. . . responds sexually to your partner's need for supportive warmth.

You may experience the confusion of emotional support something like this. One of you feels anxious, exhausted, hurt, or disappointed by events of the day and turns to the spouse for understanding and holding. You snuggle up close, yearning for the reassuring and supportive warmth of your partner. Suddenly you know your partner's response is not appropriate. You want nurturing but your partner is responding sexually.

You may withdraw angrily, feeling misunderstood and abused by your partner's sexual response to your hurting. Feeling cold and distant, you are unwilling to reach out again to your "insensitive" partner for support. You are even less willing to relate sexually.

Or you might reluctantly yield sexually in hope that after your partner is satisfied, you will receive warm, supportive holding afterward. But neither the sex nor the nurturing feels right. Sex under such circumstances makes you feel used and abused. You resent your partner's taking advantage of you sexually when you need nurturing. You are dissatisfied in your relationship with both emotional support and sex.

If you are the "insensitive" partner, you may not understand why your spouse is so disappointed and angry. After all, you were only minding your own business when your mate came snuggling up warm and intimate. You are puzzled. One moment your spouse is close and warm, the next angry and distant. You see your partner as inconsistent and confusing.

Diagnosis

When sex is confused with emotional support, neither is likely to be satisfying. They are easily confused; both can be warm, close, intimate, and physical.

But sexual relating and nurturing are sharply different. A hurting partner reaching out for emotional support is likely to feel much like an anxious, vulnerable child. A spouse seeking sex tends to feel mature, potent, and playful.

In general, men are much more likely than women to confuse nurturing with sex. In fact, some men will contend that the two are not actually different. Women rarely fail to make the distinction. Thus men are more likely to ask for sex when they actually want nurturing. Women are more likely to know the difference and to know what they want, but may nevertheless give signals confusing to men.

The confusion of sex with emotional support can cause serious marital breakdown since both are important to a satisfying relationship. Responding sexually to a need for emotional support feels unloving, even abusive. Hostile walls of frustration and resentment are erected in response to such "insensitivity." Personal support is likely to be sought and found elsewhere. Perhaps sexual fulfillment as well.

Many couples have difficulty talking about their needs and asking clearly for what is wanted. Romantic idealism that demands an accurate response without the necessity of asking can raise a barrier. Some spouses confuse themselves about their needs so that the partner cannot know how to respond. The resulting ambiguity sets the stage for misunderstanding and thus for the failure of both emotional support and sexual relating.

Prescription

The solution to such a problem is simple to explain but can be difficult for some to do. Be aware of your needs and help your partner understand them. Clarify what you want and what you don't want. Avoid the ambiguity that can make your partner feel confused and uncertain.

Ask explicitly for what you need. You can say something like: "I feel down and hurting right now, would you just hold me for a while?" Or, if there is any misunderstanding, "I'm not up for sex right now, I would just like to be held for a while."

In response to your spouse, don't assume you know what your snuggling partner wants. When in doubt, check out your assumptions. Take care not to respond sexually to a hurting spouse in need of emotional support.

Do not apologize for your needs whether for supportive holding or for sex. Both are important to the relationship but only when each is appropriate. Talk about it.

Chapter 21

When You Desire and Resist Intimacy

Symptoms

If one or more of the following descriptions seems to fit, your relationship could be enriched by this section.

One or both of you . . .

. . . yearns to feel closer to your partner.

. . . feels lonely even when together.

. . . wants to share more of your inner worlds of hopes and dreams.

. . . desires more spontaneity.

. . . hungers for the vitality of more emotional interaction.

At the same time, one or both of you . . .

. . . feels more comfortable keeping a distance.

. . . sometimes feels that "two's a crowd."

. . . preserves a private inner self.

. . . prefers formal structure to spontaneity.

. . . likes conversations to be brief and impersonal.

One of you may desire a closer relationship while the other prefers more distance.

Both of you may desire more intimacy while at the same

time feel uncomfortable when you get close.

Diagnosis

"Intimacy" is the kind of sharing and closeness that makes a relationship special. Intimacy is experienced in a variety of forms—conversational, emotional, and physical. Intimacy is much more and different than sex. A couple can have sex without intimacy and intimacy without sex.

Almost everyone yearns for intimacy—some more than others. And almost everyone fears intimacy—some more than others. People go to extraordinary measures to achieve intimacy and even more extreme efforts to avoid it.

Although both partners may want to share their lives in a close relationship, they may differ greatly in their desire for and tolerance of intimacy and how they experience or express it. One spouse may yearn longingly for the kind of closeness that the mate finds uncomfortable or difficult. What feels too close to one spouse can feel too distant to the other.

A dissatisfied spouse, longing for intimacy but married to a distant and impersonal partner, may be tempted to try to pry the partner open to pull out more self-revelation. Such efforts are rarely rewarded because a closed spouse tends to shut tighter under pressure. Intimacy, by its nature, requires a receptive, nonjudgmental, nondemanding relational climate. Thus a spouse yearning for intimacy is in a bind; neither applying pressure nor backing away is likely to produce the changes desired. The lonely partner needs to understand how difficult and uncomfortable intimate expression can be for a closed mate and to adjust expectations to reality.

The closed partner needs to be aware of the importance of intimacy to a lonely partner. Unsatisfied intimacy needs can result in serious marital dissatisfaction. Although awareness of inner thoughts and feelings and the freedom to express them may not come easily, stretching and growth are possible. A closed partner cannot expect the spouse to do all the giving when it comes to conversational or emotional expression. Additional tolerance for closeness may be needed to keep the relationship viable.

Prescription

First to spouses that yearn for more intimacy:

The bad news is that you cannot satisfy your intimacy needs by changing your partner. If you have tried, you know how frustrating that effort can be.

Understand that your nonexpressive partner is not simply stubborn or resistant, but may be genuinely blocked and unable to get in touch with and express feelings. Applying pressure to open up only reinforces the blockage. The more the pressure, the less the ability to respond. Your partner is not likely to grow and change authentically under duress.

Accept your partner "as is" without criticism or judgment. Keep remembering the qualities that first attracted you and lift them up with appreciation and affirmation.

Create a safe, affirming relational climate, free from judgment or criticism, for your spouse to experiment with self-revelation. Tell your partner about your loneliness without pressure or demands. Express appreciation for new signs of openness. Under your affirming invitation and help, your partner may get in touch with a yearning for closeness that will grow with time and nurture.

Do not allow yourself to become a "victim" of your partner, as if your happiness and fulfillment in life depended on your spouse. Do not allow yourself to become overly "needy" in your loneliness so that your inner dissatisfaction and demands escalate. Take care of yourself as your needs build. You can develop a network of intimate friends that share thoughts and feelings to help satisfy your relational needs.

Now to spouses that fear and resist relational intimacy:

Your first task is to understand the relational needs of your mate and the emptiness and disappointment when intimacy needs are not satisfied. If your spouse is lonely because of a lack of intimacy in your relationship, you will be under pressure to open up and express more of your inner world. This demand can become increasingly pressing as the needs of your partner become more urgent.

Your second task is to understand yourself. You probably feel inadequate to respond satisfactorily. You may scarcely be aware of your inner world of thoughts and feelings and even less able to express them. You are likely to recoil at an invitation to conversational or emotional intimacy.

Claim your right to be yourself. You may feel somewhat betrayed by the dissatisfaction of your mate. Your partner seemed to appreciate your quiet inner strength and emotional control earlier in your relationship. You may feel resentful; you want to be accepted again as you are.

More important, however, is that you want your spouse to be happy and satisfied in your marriage. You probably find satisfaction in the spontaneity and emotional energy of your partner even though you do not respond in kind. Your world would be drab without it.

Stretch yourself beyond your comfort zone but don't overwhelm yourself by overstating the demands. Your mate is also uneasy with intimacy to some degree. Almost everyone is. Set aside a few minutes each day for sharing. Challenge yourself to think out loud when you are together rather than sort out your thoughts privately. You can open the window to your inner world a little at a time.

In the meantime, allow your spouse to build appropriate relationships with others to satisfy these needs while you are stretching yourself.

Chapter 22

Words Don't Communicate

Symptoms

One or both of you experience frustration, lack of fulfillment, or perhaps an uncomfortable tension in a simple conversation. If you have conversations that go something like this, the issue may be yours.

    a. "Let's do something special this weekend. Just the two of us."
    b. "That might be interesting."

    a. "We need to get away, do something different. Time to be together."
    b. "I was reading an article recently that indicated that weekends away together can benefit a marriage."

    a. "See! So what would you like to do this weekend?"
    b. "This article indicated that the kind of weekend away that works for one couple may not work for another."

    a. "Right. So what kind of weekend will work for you and me?"
    b. "Of course, partners in a relationship may have different preferences when it comes to planning a weekend."

a. "So, what would be your preference?"

b. "If couples don't agree, it may work better to maintain familiar routines rather than end up doing something they cannot enjoy together."

a. "Right. So let's do something we both would like. What would you enjoy?"

b. "Some people seem to prefer active weekends like hiking, climbing, fishing, or searching for antiques."

a. "So would you like to do something physical this weekend?"

b. "On the other hand, some prefer simply to relax, eat, read, sleep, no responsibilities."

a. "We could just go somewhere and collapse. Would you like that?"

b. "There are benefits to each. It all depends on the individuals and what they want . . ."

You are not likely to enjoy this kind of conversation indefinitely. One partner feels frustrated, unable to make real contact and find out what the partner feels and wants. The other feels under pressure to open up and reveal personal preferences at an uncomfortable level.

Diagnosis

Every conversation has a level of intimacy—some higher, some lower. Five levels of intimacy in a conversation might be identified from lowest to highest as follows.

1. Intellectual data or facts.
2. Opinions and ideas of people you both know.
3. Your own opinions and ideas.
4. Your personal emotions, preferences, yearnings.
5. Feelings about "you and me, here and now."

In the conversation above, one partner attempts to draw the other into a higher level of intimacy (level 4). The other resists, keeping the discussion impersonal, intellectual, offering little self-revelation (level 1). The greater the difference between intimacy levels, the greater the disappointment and/or discomfort with the conversation.

The partner wanting more intimacy is likely to feel frustrated and unfulfilled, hearing what the partner thinks but not what is personally felt or wanted. The more the partner talks, the less is revealed. Additional pressure to become more personal is likely to produce only more intellectualizing.

A partner that feels under pressure to disclose personal feelings often reacts, usually without awareness, by building a wall of words and facts for protection. The more the pressure, the thicker the wall. Intellectualizing can be an alternative to or an escape from intimacy.

Thus the conversation above is frustrating, uncomfortable, and dissatisfying to both partners. Each partner talks at a different level of intimacy. Pressure and resistance replaces genuine sharing.

Effective communication requires couples to talk at satisfying levels of personal sharing. To achieve this, partners need to be aware of the level of intimacy in their conversations and accept and adjust to each other's needs and fears.

Prescription

Be aware when you are missing each other by talking on different levels. Be aware of pulling or pushing away when frustrated or uncomfortable at the level of intimacy in a conversation. The "Levels of Intimacy" listed above can help you know what you can do to raise or lower it.

Stretch yourself to enjoy conversations at different levels of intimacy. All levels can be enjoyable but not always to the same degree. Intellectual discussions are preferred by some just as intimate conversations are more fulfilling to others. One is not necessarily better or worse. Although most couples enjoy some conversation at each level, most partners need at least some communication at the higher levels of intimacy to keep a relationship close and special.

Your own and your spouse's desire and tolerance for intimacy will not always, perhaps ever, be the same. One of you may yearn for intimate conversations with the same passion that the other avoids them. Do not attempt to change your partner to become like yourself. However, the more you accept yourself and your mate as you are, the more change and growth is likely to occur.

If you are the partner wanting more self-disclosure, you need to provide a safe, accepting climate least likely to produce resistance. Unlike the conversation above, the partner with the desire for self-disclosure needs to take the initiative when talking about personal desires and preferences. Attempting to draw out the partner is understandable but usually futile. Intimacy is more likely achieved in a conversational climate free from pressure.

If your partner's tolerance for intimacy is too limited for your needs, you may have to find intimate conversations elsewhere so that resentment does not mount up and undermine the intimacy that may be possible.

If you are the partner that is less comfortable with personal self-disclosure, you need to understand the needs of your mate and how words can both reveal or conceal. You may not be willing or able to sustain conversations at the highest level of intimacy as outlined above, but you can move up a step or two when needed.

If your partner's yearning for intimate conversation exceeds your tolerance limits, encourage your mate to find other appropriate companions who can help satisfy this need. Intimate conversations with friends outside of your marriage supply a need to which you cannot comfortably respond.

Chapter 23

You Want Emotional Intimacy

Symptoms

You or your partner yearn for more emotional expression in your relationship, to be more playful, to share your inner hopes and fears, to vent your anger, and, perhaps, at times, to cry together. If one of the following statements fit, this section might be able to help.

You or your partner . . .

. . . feels lonely and out of contact with your spouse, almost like living with a stranger.

. . . buries your feelings convinced that expressing them is a waste of time and energy.

. . . disguises your emotions; for example, you cry when you are angry, smile when you are sad, act tough when you are scared, or get angry when you are hurting.

. . . expresses controlling emotions such as anger but not "weaker" ones like sadness or fear.

. . . allows yourself to express vulnerable emotions such as fear or sadness but retreats from expressing anger.

One of you vents emotion easily while the other seems unable to identify or express feelings.

One of you feels most alive and connected when interacting emotionally while the other feels threatened and uncomfortable when feelings are expressed.

Diagnosis

Couples talk to each other with both "words and music," that is, with both verbal content and emotion.

Both lyrics and music, both words and emotions, are useful and necessary for satisfying communication in marriage. Words without emotion work well to define, analyze, and solve problems. Emotional expression is needed to achieve that special kind of closeness many yearn to experience in marriage.

Some partners only hear and understand words while others listen and respond to the music, that is, to underlying feelings. For some spouses, human interaction without emotion is like a world without music—dull, drab, boring, and empty. Other spouses live more comfortably in a world without emotion, and, in fact, may be unaware of their feelings, unable to identify them, or give them appropriate expression.

If one partner focuses on feelings while the other attends only to literal content, conversations will break down as when different languages are spoken. Spouses need to understand and appreciate the "language" of their mates and to learn in time to speak it. One spouse may need to pay more attention to the meaning of words while the other needs to respond more to feelings.

Thus some partners may need to tone down the music and attend more thoughtfully to the literal content of their own and their partner's words to achieve more satisfying interaction. They need to use words to convey meaning rather than to evoke an emotional response. Such thoughtful restraint may not come easily, especially when emotional closeness is pressingly needed.

More often, partners need to grow in awareness of feelings and their ability to identify and express them. This task can be difficult. But the reward of a stable, satisfying, and close relationship makes the challenge worth facing.

For some "strong silent types," identifying and expressing feelings can be like learning a new language in a foreign culture. One way to practice the language of feelings is to identify four basic emotions of which all others are variations or combinations. Although different words can be used to describe each of them depending on intensity, they are:

1. *Fear* (Anxiety, uneasiness, etc.)
2. *Sadness* (Disappointment, grief, etc.)
3. *Anger* (Resentment, indignation, etc.)
4. *Joy* (Contentment, excitement, etc.)

These four emotions are experienced in almost every situation in varying proportions. Spouses with difficulty identifying and expressing emotion can challenge themselves to express each of them in describing an experience. For example, as this is written, I might express anxiety (fear) at a possible waste of an enormous investment of time and resources in producing this book, regret (sadness) over what cannot be included, irritation (anger) over printing and publishing hassles, and excitement (joy) over the potential helpfulness of the work. All four can be identified, although anxiousness and excitement are on top at this point.

Spouses with controlled personalities often protest: "Yes, but what good does it do to express feelings? Venting emotions doesn't change anything!" Not true. Expressing feelings between spouses helps to build a close, supportive, and satisfying relationship. If practical action is needed, that comes later.

Some spouses seem able to express some feelings but not others, for example, resentment but not sadness, fear but not anger. Expressing only one feeling, like listening to one piece of music, can become monotonous. Communication is limited and predictable. The words and music get out of sync. Inner worlds remain mostly hidden.

Music and lyrics need to match. Effective communication and emotional intimacy requires that words and feelings be congruent, for example, tears for sadness, anger when resentful, and anxiousness when fearful. Confused messages are sent and understanding breaks down when resentment is expressed with tears, hurt with anger, or fear with toughness.

Without the "music" of emotion, a relationship can become dissatisfying for spouses who yearn for and need emotional interaction. A conversation without feeling can convey information, sort alternatives, and make objectively considered decisions, but it cannot build satisfying intimacy.

Prescription

Determine to listen to and express both words and feelings. All communication has some "music," however disguised, muted, or hidden. Conversely, important content can be found in emotional expression no matter how irrational the words may seem.

Challenge yourself to express appropriate emotion and to invite and receive the feelings of your partner. You can help each other expand your range and congruence. If your partner is receptive, you can give helpful feedback such as: "You sound resentful, but I think you are also sad and disappointed." Or, "I know you are crying, but you also sound angry." You can enrich your emotional intimacy by expressing feelings accurately with vitality and color.

If you are married to a "strong, silent type" who has difficulty expressing emotion or understanding your feelings, do not attempt to build intimacy by pulling out emotion as if you were pulling teeth. Emotional intimacy requires an accepting climate free from pressure and resistance. You will have more success by modeling emotional openness, by helping your partner to understand your needs, and by providing time and opportunity for sharing.

Basic Steps for Enriching Emotional Intimacy

The following basic steps for enriching emotional intimacy is for the "strong silent type" that tends to have difficulty identifying or expressing feelings. You get uneasy when a conversation becomes emotional. You may appreciate emotional vitality in your spouse, but become uncomfortable, confused, and defensive when under pressure to express your own. At times you may be convinced that you have no feelings to express.

You know that sharing feelings is important to your spouse. The lack of emotional interaction causes your partner to feel lonely and dissatisfied with your marriage. You don't want to lose your mate or your marriage but you feel uncomfortable and incompetent when it comes to emotional intimacy. If you are ready and willing to take action, here is some help.

Challenge yourself to expand your comfort zone. Don't withdraw as quickly when a conversation becomes emotional. Take the risk of responding out of your own emotions. You may feel empty inside at first when you probe for your feelings. Nevertheless, you have emotions churning inside; you only need to get in touch with them. Here are three steps that can help you.

1. Practice awareness. Pay attention to your body. Tight muscles. A nervous movement. A burning inside. Exhaustion. A restless discomfort. Be aware of thoughts relating to what your body is doing. Push yourself to talk about these thoughts and sensations.

2. Identify the feelings you connect with your thoughts and sensations. Make an informed guess if you don't know what you feel. If you cannot identify your feelings, check your thoughts and sensations against the four basic emo-

tions: fear, sadness, anger, or joy.

3. Express the feelings you have identified in an appropriate way. Be alert and receptive to similar feelings in your spouse.

If you are getting in touch with emotions for the first time, you might be like a color-blind person beginning to see colors. A new world opens up with new possibilities requiring a new vocabulary. As you become aware of your feelings and able to identify them, you need to learn to find words and ways to express them so that you achieve the desired level of emotional intimacy. Don't demand instant success; give yourself plenty of time to practice and learn.

If an inability to identify or name your feelings persists, here is an exercise that can give you practice. Learn the four basic emotions from memory: fear, sadness, anger, and joy. Challenge yourself to identify each of the four feelings in describing recent experiences in your life. You may need to use a little imagination at first.

You might begin by challenging yourself to use all four of the basic emotions as you describe to your spouse your emotional reaction to this book. Here is some help. You might find yourself saying something like:

1. "I feel a kind of *fear* (anxiousness, anxiety, etc.) inside when pressed to deal with feelings; I do not feel comfortable or adequate with emotions.

2. "I feel *sad* (disappointed, wistful, etc.) at the thought of changing; I am familiar and comfortable with the way I am."

3. "Actually, I get *angry* (resentful, irritated, etc.) at pressures to open up and express emotions; I want to be accepted the way I am."

4. "I can feel some *joy* (excitement, hopefulness, etc.) when I think of building a closer and more satisfying marriage relationship."

Learning to surface, identify, and appropriately express your emotions may seem difficult or even impossible but the rewards to your marriage and all of life can be enormous.

Chapter 24

When You Want More Touching

Description

If one or more of the statements below fit, this chapter is designed to help.

You or your partner . . .

. . . yearn for more touching in addition to and apart from your sexual relating.

. . . would like additional warm, supportive holding in the morning when you wake or at night before you sleep.

. . . would like a more satisfying pattern of hugs and kisses with "good-bye's" and "hello's" when leaving or returning.

. . . want more touching when sitting together, i.e., holding hands, head in the lap, arms around shoulders, etc.

. . . want more mutual body care, i.e., back, foot, or whole body massages.

One of you feels at ease with prolonged physical touching while the other feels uncomfortable.

One of you experiences touching as a basic everyday human need while the other limits it to special romantic moments or sexual contact.

Diagnosis

Everyone needs to be touched. There is reason to believe that people who receive adequate physical affection tend to live longer and healthier than those who don't.

Some spouses seem to want or need more touching than others. Some never seem to get enough; others are uncomfortable with physical closeness.

Physical affection can be particularly helpful for building a healthy self-image. Touching and holding tend to convey unconditionally that a partner is lovable.

Spouses need to tell their mates the kind of touching they enjoy: running fingers through hair; playing footsies under the table; light tingly rubbing; stroking selective parts of the body (hair, forehead, back, feet, etc.); solid bear hugs or tender embraces; entwining fingers; walking arm in arm, hand in hand, or arms around waists or shoulders; secret touches in public situations, etc.

Partners also need to know and respond to their mate's preferred kinds of touching. Spouses cannot assume their partners will always like what they themselves enjoy.

Not all touching feels good or helps. Touching that is abrasive, excessive, or coercive can be destructive to a relationship. Partners need to tell each other when touching does not feel good and expect the other to stop abruptly on request. Physical intimacy requires a relational climate free from pressure or demands.

Sometimes touching that seems tender and affectionate to one partner may be uncomfortable or even abusive to the other. Childhood experiences often account for such differences. A satisfying physical intimacy requires sharing and respecting these individual differences.

Partners whose spouses want more physical touching than they can comfortably provide need to understand their spouses's needs and the mutual benefit of satisfying them. With sufficient motivation, effort, and patience, tolerance for

physical touching can be expanded to the benefit and fulfillment of both spouses.

Prescription

Be aware of your need and desire for physical touching.
Let yourself know what feels good and what does not. Don't
expect your partner to know your needs unless you talk
about them.

Be aware of your partner's need and desire for physical
touching. Learn to know what feels good to your partner
and what does not. If you think you already know, check out
your assumptions.

If you have difficulty with physical touching, explore
inner blocks that might prevent you from knowing and
expressing your needs or attending to those of your partner.
You may feel uncomfortable when physically close for
reasons you have not fully explored. Do you disown parts of
your body that you have come to dislike? Do you feel some-
how unworthy of physical affection? Do you take a self-
defeating pride in imagining yourself to be above such
needs? Do you anticipate rejection if you are too close, too
long?

Check such feelings or assumptions against reality by discussing them with your mate. Then determine to give yourself whatever inner permission you may need to touch and
be touched whenever, wherever, however, and as long as it
feels good or helpful.

Tell your mate what rituals of touching you prefer when
leaving or returning home or when waking up or going to
sleep. Ask what patterns of touching your partner prefers.

If you are able to give and receive touching easily but
your spouse prefers physical distance, learn to accept and
respect this "differentness." Do not attempt to pressure your
partner into closeness. Crowding a reluctant partner with
demands for physical closeness tends to reinforce the desire

for distance. You would do better to express your needs without complaining or demanding while providing safe, accepting opportunities conducive to being close.

Do not allow yourself to become overly "needy" so that you respond to your partner with frustration fueled by desperation. Find acceptable sources to satisfy your need for nonsexual physical touching outside of your marriage that your partner cannot satisfy such as with extended family, nurturing organizations, or appropriate friends.

If you have a partner that needs more nonsexual touching than you can comfortably give, consider stretching yourself. Although you may have to push beyond your comfort limits, you could benefit personally as well as enrich your marriage.

Let yourself know how you create distance when you are getting too close for comfort. You may be:

1. Pushing away—with words or actions
2. Pulling away—withdraw mentally or physically
3. Tuning out—block inwardly

As you become aware of how you create distance, you can challenge yourself to stretch a little beyond your normal tolerance. As you expand your comfort limits for prolonged touching, you are likely to benefit mentally, emotionally, and physically as well as relationally. You may even come to enjoy it.

Do not allow yourself to become defensive or jealous if your spouse satisfies unmet needs by finding people who touch and hug nonsexually among family or friends. Make it your goal to understand your mate, encourage efforts to satisfy this need outside your marriage, and respond by satisfying more of this need yourself.

Chapter 25

You Want More Intimacy in Sex

Symptoms

If the level of closeness and sharing in your sexual relating is an issue in your marriage, one or more of the following statements probably apply.

One or both of you . . .

. . . finds your sexual relating too predictable, lacking in spontaneity.

. . . experiences your sexual relating as overly physical, lacking a full range of mental, emotional, or spiritual involvement.

. . . feels that sex is too much "by the book," more attentive to technique than to the partner.

. . . finds your sexual expression to be overly casual, lacking intensity of involvement.

. . . experiences your sexual relating to be somewhat coercive; one demands, the other yields.

. . . sometimes experiences sexual relating as an obligation.

. . . sometimes grants or withholds sex in order to reward or to punish.

. . . feels that your partner desires sex in general not you in particular.

. . . frequently yearns to make love that is more enjoyable, relational, or fun.

Diagnosis

Sexual relations for most couples is not consistently intimate in the sense that spouses share thoughts and emotion as well as body parts. Types of nonintimate sex include:

Mechanical sex
Ritual sex
Recreational sex
Manipulative sex
Obligatory sex
Animal or "raunchy" sex
Sex in exchange for something
Acting out unexpressed sexual fantasies.

Most spouses enjoy a variety of kinds of sex when the mood and inclination is conducive. And all kinds may have a place. But most partners will be disappointed if sexual relating is not genuinely intimate some, if not most, of the time.

Genuinely intimate sex is free from pressures and resistance. No one coerces and no one is compelled; no one scores and no one is scored upon.

Intimate sex is spontaneous. Partners are genuinely and expressively themselves, sharing their inner worlds of thoughts and feelings, yearnings and fantasies, likes and dislikes without fear of judgment. Intimate sex has a childlike quality, open to explore, experience, ask, and respond with uncensored curiosity and delight. It is built on a relational climate of uninhibited openness, free from pressures or demands, that says expectantly: "Let's see what happens if we get sexy with each other."

Such intimacy is difficult to achieve for some couples.

Both partners need to be able to tolerate prolonged and genuine closeness. They need to be able to convey what is wanted and what is not wanted without pressure or resistance—something many spouses find particularly difficult. Sexual intimacy requires an accepting, uncritical, nondefensive emotional climate free from performance expectations. While partners will not always get what they want, they need to be free to express any desire without fear of ridicule.

Tolerance of sexual intimacy can differ greatly between partners. One spouse may enjoy extended closeness of body, mind, emotions, and spirit before, during, and following intercourse. The other may be uncomfortable with extended closeness, focus more narrowly on the genitals, and withdraw rapidly after orgasm. Such differences need to be understood and accepted so that both can grow in willingness to adjust to the needs of the other.

Efforts to pressure a spouse or yourself to perform sexually tends to exacerbate and complicate sexual problems. Sexual relating that is demanded tends to become burdensome. Unrealistic expectations of yourself or your partner can create "performance anxiety" interfering with sexual responses. Spouses who think of sexual relating as conquering or surrendering are sometimes defeated by "control anxiety" in which intimacy is replaced by competition. The tension between demands and resistance prevents some spouses from feeling free to "let go" physically and emotionally.

Prescription

Explore your sexual preferences before considering changes. Identify from the list of nonintimate sex types above some of the ways that you tend to relate sexually. Let yourself know which ones you prefer.

Be aware of the satisfactions and benefits you derive from

nonintimate sex, such as reducing anxiety, fantasy fulfillment, reduced intensity, energy conservation, avoiding
rejection, high excitement, rapid release, or maintaining control.

Determine whether you want more or less intimacy in
your sexual relating. If you want to increase your level of
sexual intimacy at least part of the time, here are some suggestions:

1. Approach your partner without demands or expectations of any kind. Allow your partner to be free to respond
or not to respond in any way.

2. Do not make your partner responsible for your sexual
fulfillment. Be aware of your own needs. Feel free to ask for
what you want but allow your partner equal freedom in
response. Your partner is not responsible for your orgasm.

3. Do not take responsibility for your partner's sexual fulfillment. You do not need to perform for your partner; you
only need to enjoy. You are not responsible for your partner's orgasm.

4. Tell your partner what feels good and what does not.
Do not expect your partner to know what you want without
asking. Don't do something to your partner in order to get
the same done to you; it rarely works that way. Take care
that your requests do not sound like demands; allow your
partner to respond freely, yes or no. You will not achieve
intimacy by making demands.

5. Ask your partner to tell you what feels good and what
does not. Don't expect your partner to enjoy a sexual act
just because you do. Don't assume you know what your
partner likes; expect some sexual surprises from your partner no matter how long you have been married.

6. Develop the kind of playful childlikeness that can
explore, experience and enjoy freely, talk openly, invite and
respond without demands, expectations, judgment, or constraints.

If you have a partner who finds prolonged intimacy uncomfortable, avoid clutching beyond your mate's comfort zone. Holding too close for too long can add to resistance and increase a desire for distance. Instead, provide a warm, accepting, comfortable emotional climate which allows your partner to respond free from pressure.

If you have a spouse who wants prolonged sexual intimacy that is beyond your tolerance level, make an effort to understand your partner's need. You may become aware of similar yearnings hidden within yourself. Stretch yourself to prolong foreplay, delay climax, and extend the warmth and closeness of the after-burn. Press yourself each time to stay close a little beyond your comfort zone. You can expand your tolerance for a more total and prolonged sexual intimacy that might satisfy some of your own hidden needs as well as those of your partner.

Building a satisfying level of sexual intimacy can be difficult if you have diverse tolerance levels, but you have a lot to gain for yourself, your partner, and your marriage in the process.

Chapter 26
You Feel Out of Love

Symptoms

This last chapter is for you if you sometimes feel that you are no longer in love, that your marriage may be a mistake.

It can happen even before your wedding. High on romance, you wonder what is real and what is fantasy. You are eager to please. You are not altogether your real self as you try to fulfill your partner's expectations. You realize that your image of your partner is partly your own romantic creation. You doubt, at times, that you genuinely know and love the real person you are going to marry.

It can happen early in marriage as you descend from your romantic high, no longer idealize your partner, face your real differences, surface your conflicts, and deal with everyday tensions. The excitement of your relationship dissolves into adjustment and effort. Love seems gone.

It can happen after years of marriage. The limits and restrictions of marriage no longer feel comfortable. You want freedom to come and go as you please, expand other relationships, and experiment with new ones. Your spouse seems to stand in the way of your restless yearning rather than fulfilling it. Love seems gone.

It can happen later in marriage and in life. You become independent emotionally and/or financially. Your marriage no longer seems needed for your children or yourself. You may yearn to be free from dependency on your spouse or from having your spouse dependent on you. Daily routine becomes deadeningly familiar. You may yearn for something more and different that can revitalize your life. Your partner belongs to the past, not the future. Love seems gone.

Love can also disappear if you become attracted to someone who interests and excites you more than your spouse. You want to be free to build an exciting relationship that gives life new color and makes you feel young again. Vitality seems to lie with your new love; dull, repetitious role-playing with your spouse. Love seems gone—at least toward your spouse.

Whatever the reason, season, or circumstances for feeling out of love, you may be convinced that when love dies, marriage is dead. You may be determined not to spend the rest of your life in a loveless marriage.

On the other hand, you may have a spouse who has come to feel out of love with you. You feel confused, rejected, perhaps devastated. You may try to cling tightly to your spouse. Or you may turn away, push away, or run away from the "unloving" partner. You feel betrayed. You fear that love is gone forever.

Diagnosis

All of the feelings described above are normal and predictable as part of married life.

All spouses fall out of love at times. If you have never fallen out of love with your spouse, you may be a rare exception or you may not want to admit those feelings even to yourself. Falling in and out of love with a mate is the normal course of marital relating. Married partners sometimes feel

loving, sometimes feel unloving or even hostile, and sometimes feel almost nothing at all.

Partners are most likely to feel out of love at transitional
junctures of their life. An early transition comes when idealized romantic infatuation deflates into dealing with the challenges and conflicts of everyday life. Loving feelings can dis-
solve in the heat of adult pressures and demands. Tensions
can grind loving feelings down when the idealized image of
a partner dissolves into a real person with a contrasting set
of preferences, attitudes, thoughts, feelings, values, needs,
and wants. Disappointment at the loss of the excitement of
romance needs to be overcome so that new, deeper, and
more mature levels of relating can develop.

The now familiar "mid-life crisis" can be another transition that puts stress on marriages. Familiar values, priorities,
life-style preferences, loyalties, and other fundamentals of
life are questioned. Marital commitment seems more confining than reassuring. Experimentation with new possibilities
becomes exciting. Marriage often seems to stand in the way
of new beginnings. Exploring new relationships can become
important. Love for the spouse may seem to belong to the
past, not to the future. Yet, even when turbulent, this time of
readjustment can be an opportunity for vital growth in a
marital relationship. Marriages, like individuals, need to
grow and change with life's stages.

Transitional periods can also occur when either partner is
making personal or life changes, as, for example, from
housekeeping to a career, or from a salaried position to self-
employment, or from work to retirement. Such transitions
require adjustments in role expectations. The partner left
behind by a changing mate may feel neglected, even
abandoned. The partner on the move outgrows the static
partner. One moves on, the other holds back. Feelings of
love are strained in the tension.

Being out-of-love is normal and can be expected in every

long-term relationship. Over the course of a lifetime, almost every married person would sometimes like to be married to a different partner. Although about half of all marriages end in divorce, virtually all partners consider it at one time or another—although many would not admit it even to themselves. If occasionally feeling out of love indicates that a marriage is unhealthy, there are no sound marriages.

A love recession in your relationship can be a springboard to new stages of growing and loving. A loss of love signals a time to stop and look at what is happening in a marriage. When one partner feels out of love, the spouse probably also feels at least vaguely dissatisfied. Marriages, like all living things, need to grow to survive. Couples that have been married for many years often look back at those "out of love" experiences as important new beginnings that brought new vitality to their relationship.

Feeling out of love can be a helpful experience when accepted as normal, faced honestly, and understood as an invitation to make enriching changes in marriage.

Prescription

When you feel out of love, don't do anything rash. Accept feeling out-of-love as normal and healthy in your marriage.

Explore your feelings. Examine honestly what is going on—or not going on—in your marriage. Be aware of any yearnings or fantasies that might provide clues to what you really want. For example, you may want to break out of routine, have more fun, get high on romance, explore new relationships, or claim freedom to move with your impulses.

Don't protect your spouse from your feelings. Although telling your partner about your feeling out of love may be initially threatening, acting on your feelings without talking is worse. You are likely to discover that your partner also yearns for something new, better, or different in your relationship.

Tell yourself that a love recession is a helpful signal that your relationship needs redefinition. You may need more separateness from your partner so that you can rediscover and reclaim your individuality. You may need more adventure, more excitement, more freedom, more life.

Experiment with new behavior. Break relational habits that seem stale or rutted. Give yourself freedom to try something new. You may be ready for a new hobby, change of jobs, go back to school, or build some new and different kinds of friendships. Do not allow yourself to feel trapped or suffocated in your marriage.

Take new risks with your partner. Feeling out-of-love can free you to become more self-revealing, share your dreams, and express your emotions. Try expressing thoughts and feelings you usually hide. Claim more personal freedom if that is what you want and need. Don't play a role that has become oppressive. If you tend to be over-adaptive, become more assertive or vice versa. Invite your partner to share in some of your yearnings and fantasies.

Let feeling out-of-love free you to try what you have not dared before. Try new activities, i.e., join a theater group, run for political office, join a health club, or develop your spirituality. Don't use marital constraints as an excuse to retreat from the life you yearn to live.

Receive your out-of-love feelings as a gift to you, to your partner, and to your marriage. Make it a time to break stale patterns and to make a fresh start. Let your love recession restore a sense of uncertainty and adventure to your relationship.

Keep this book handy for suggesting issues and directions for building, rebuilding, renewing, or reshaping your relationship when you feel out of love.

Chapter 27

For Further Consideration

Taken as whole, there are few if any richer gifts or more rewarding achievements in human life than a successful, satisfying marriage.

And there are few, if any, more difficult challenges. A successful marriage requires much more than avoiding separation or divorce. Most unhappy marriages endure resulting in lifelong misery.

Although always important and sometimes essential, love and commitment are not enough for a satisfying relationship. Among qualities also needed:

1. Awareness of significant differences between partners.
2. Relational and problem-solving skills.
3. Sensitivity and responsiveness to personal needs.
4. Availability, openness, and, at times, vulnerability.

Even more is needed. You need to accept your partner and your marriage "as is" and to build a satisfying life within the limits of the possible. No marriage partner will ever measure up to your ideal—no matter how many spouses you have. No marriage will ever measure up to your ideal—no matter how many times you marry. You need to make peace with yourself between your ideal expectations and the limits imposed by reality.

It can help to have a perspective that appreciates the building of a successful marriage as a crowning achievement. When the subtleties are understood in depth, a short-lived romance, however passionate, is less interesting, challenging, dramatic, or ultimately rewarding as the most prosaic marriage.

A problem-free marriage is not an option. Successful marriages have the same problems faced by others. The difference is only that successful marriages tend to face and resolve problems successfully.

This book was written to help you do just that. It was not written to be read from cover and cover and discarded. If you have read through the book, you are ready to go back and identify the areas in your marriage that need further exploration. Read those sections again reflecting in more depth on your relationship.

Keep this book as a reference for further use. Marriages tend to have plateaus of stability between periods of growth and change. You can return to this book again and again to deal with marital issues at deeper levels as your relationship grows toward higher levels of maturity.